Happiness in Your Relation- ships and Systemic Family Constellation Work

Live a fulfilling partner rela- tionship with love and respect

Marc Baco

Note

This publication has been researched and composed to our best knowledge. The author and the publisher are not liable for ideas, concepts, recommendations and statements found herein.

The published advice and tips are intended to help readers form their own conclusions and resolutions.

Please contact your physician, health care provider or therapist with any further questions.

The author and the publisher cannot guarantee personal solutions. In all cases you are responsible for your actions.

We wish to clearly point out to you, the reader of this book, that we do not guarantee or promise any success, personal desired outcome, or anything else. Moreover, we are not liable for any aftermath that might occur to the reader in connection with the content of this book.

The reader is responsible for any ideas and actions that he or she might take as a result of reading this book.

Contents

Introduction

Anyone who has read my first published book *Stopping the Obesity Pattern with Family Systemic Constellation Work* will find some familiar passages in this book, since the topic of "interrupted movement toward a parent" can show up as a symptom when addressing obesity or lack of money, as well as relationship problems.

Relationship problems can have many causes and reasons.

Sometime the reason is just a lack of education. Even though we learn many subjects in school, how to manage a relationship is not among them, unfortunately.

Accordingly, relationship guides and self-help books are by far the most numerous of published books in the nonfiction genre. The majority of these books give very useful tips on how you can improve the quality of your personal relationships. But only on rare occasions are root causes of the issues addressed.

Suppose you have a serious relationship problem. Picture this problem as a heavy knight's helmet with a visor. The visor has only two narrow slits through which you can perceive the world. Most relationship self-help books will give you tips on how to extend your field of vision through clever head movements, or how to strengthen your neck muscles so you can carry the weight of the helmet more easily. They offer you mental exercises so that you can accept the helmet as part of your life with the restrictions that it entails.

However, this book is intended to prepare you to finally remove the helmet, allowing you an unobstructed view of your partner. This leads to a relaxation in your neck, since you no longer need to bear the weight of the helmet. Now you have the freedom to really meet each other in your relationship.

Family systemic constellation work is a very open system that easily integrates findings from other fields of study such as psychology, other forms of therapy, or coaching. Therefore, I will discuss in a later chapter some basic features of Transactional Analysis, the Drama Triangle and other approaches in neighboring areas that also play a role in family constellation work.

First, however, we will deal with some basic insights into family constellation work that apply to a successful partnership.

At this point, I have to reject scientific theories that demand reproducibility and verifiable hypotheses. Family constellation work as I know and practice it doesn't fulfill these requirements. It remains a phenomenological therapy with an esoteric touch.

That means that I will probably not reach those readers who have a solely scientific worldview.

Yes, I can't provide evidence and most likely your concern is so individual that the findings of this book are only a guide and in no way replace a family systemic constellation.

Therefore, this book is directed toward family constellation practitioners and interested laymen who want to work with personal relationship issues, and for whom a family constellation is the best way to tackle these challenges.

Marc Baco, Family Systemic Constellation Facilitator in Freiburg im Breisgau, Germany

Systemic Thinking — the Logic of the Family System

Why me? Why do I always struggle with relationship problems, but not my brother or sister?

Have you perhaps asked yourself this question before? And you didn't come to a satisfying answer?

In order to avoid presenting all of the theory of family constellations, I will summarize it somewhat loosely. The family system usually enlists only one member of the family to draw attention to an imbalance. It creates a blind compensation, which means that the chosen family member has not been found guilty of anything similar, nor is he or she particularly suitable for solving the issue — it is absolutely arbitrary and random.

Thus the family system creates a stable equilibrium — at the expense of an individual.

In persecutor-victim-context, this principle is particularly easy to identify.

For example, in order to point out the wrongdoing of his grandfather who had denounced a Communist during the Nazi era (which led to the Communist's death), the grandchild can innocently be accused — on a trip to the U.S. — of murder, and end up in prison on death row. Although the grandson doesn't know of his grandfather's deed, the family system uses him to point it out.

A second elementary principle is that suppressed or not fully lived emotions have a very destructive effect on a person and their environment. For example, grief that is not expressed to its completion can cause similar relationship problems like suppressed anger. More about this in the individual chapters.

All these phenomena are located in the system of the family or in the system or the psyche of the client. Both systems are supported and helped by family constellation work. And both systems — separately or together — can hamper the success of a partnership tremendously.

Insights about Partnerships through Family Constellation Work

When a man and woman become a couple, two different family systems are brought together. Mostly the problems of the couple do not stem from their relationship itself, but from entanglements and effects of the original family systems of each partner.

On a deeper level, the partners meet in order to mutually mirror their problem areas to each other, and work through it together. This then leads to intellectual and spiritual growth, as long as the couple accepts this challenge consciously.

According to Bert Hellinger, a husband and wife gift the respective energies of their poles to each other, because each needs the other. The woman gives the man his feminine side, while the man gives the woman her masculine aspect. A problem arises when each doesn't truly embrace their own pole, or systemic influences prevent the partners from living in a healthy relationship.

To embrace and live one's respective gender requires a healthy relationship with the same-sex parent (daughter to mother, son to father) or even better, a healthy relationship with the whole same-sex lineage. Here interferences can blatantly obstruct the ability to bond, and in the long run prevent the experience of nourishing, fulfilling relationships.

In constellations the facilitator often sets up a so-called line of ancestors to regain full manhood or womanhood. This ancestral line shows, for example, a generational model to a female client, with her mother behind her, then her grandmother, and the great grandmother, etc.

The experience of the flow of the feminine power through the generations can be very beneficial and lead to a balanced, genuine female force that does not need to rise above masculinity because it rests in itself.

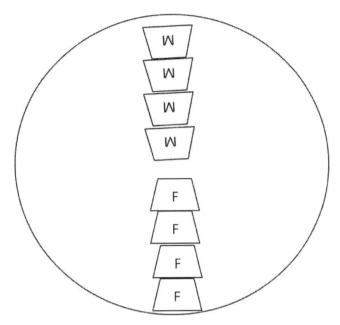

Figure 1: Ancestral Lineage of the Couple

In practical terms, the ancestral line can be set up by having the ancestors on the outside put their arms on the shoulders of later generations and so on. When a couple meets each other with their ancestral line in back of them, everyone is aligned on their pole and besides the sexual dynamic there is a sense of healthy exchange and balancing of give and take (see the corresponding chapter below).

In principle, men and women are equal and the same. They are on the same hierarchical level. The partner who earns more money is usually granted the place on the right — regardless of whether this is the man or the woman. Here the only thing that counts is who earns more in a job outside of the relationship and thus is contributing more financially. There is no fixed rule that, for example, the man must always be on the right side when the partners are next to each other in a constellation. In addition, it's better that the partner who is less burdened by their family system is standing to the right, because they can shoulder more.

There has been some controversy and raised eyebrows about Bert Hellinger's observation that it's better for the couple when "the woman follows the man and the man in return serves the feminine." Here the term 'follow' means to accompany the man into his culture, country, family, etc. Conversely, if the man follows the woman into her culture, failure is inevitable.

I pass this insight by Hellinger on for the sake of being complete. He has made more than 10,000 constellations and I just over 500. Please feel free to form an opinion yourself.

Create a new, shared value system

Therefore a man will leave his father and his mother, and will join with his wife, and they will be one flesh. Genesis 2:24 (*World English Bible*)

At the very beginning of the Bible, the couple is asked to leave the values of the family (in a figurative sense) and to create a new system of values for themselves ("They will be one flesh"). For the success of the relationship they must re-evaluate their own values and principles, and together they negotiate new ones. This is called the Relationship Vision. Mostly this happens after the honeymoon phase, when the partners meet each other without the rose-colored glasses and the couple hits the first bumps in the road.

The importance of love in family constellations

Although it isn't shouted from the rooftops, love is given the highest importance and priority in family constellations.

What interests us here in particular is the love between man and woman.

This often shows up indirectly. If parents who don't love each other have children, the children suffer greatly from the lack of love of their parents through entanglements and dynamics of all kinds.

On the other hand, I have observed that the children of parents with a strong loving bond experience less entanglements and unhealthy dynamics.

The healthy love is based on mutual respect, on equality, on recognition and appreciation of the other gender, and the affectionate balance of give and take.

That, of course, includes not wanting to change the partner and being willing to accompany them at their pace in their development.

The shared experience of maturation in one's own personality and of the relationship will deepen through the experience of daily togetherness.

This also includes the important systemic principle that everyone has to carry their own destiny. It is a sign of true love to not take on the partner's burdens and relieve them of their fate. This leaves the other in humility all their dignity.

Useful Insights and Influences From Outside the Family Constellation Approach

Family constellation work, as it is understood by the new Freiburg School, is a very open-minded system that incorporates NLP (neuro-linguistic programming) for useful outside influences. My instructor Wolfgang Bracht has always encouraged us to integrate new methods into family constellation work and test them to the extent that they are helpful and healing.

The advanced protective layer model according to Trobe

One of the models that complements family constellation work is the protective layer model by Dr. Thomas Trobe, which I like to present in a version that I have slightly altered. Basically, it is a kind of inner child work.

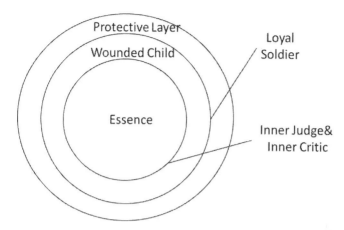

Figure 2: Protective Layer Model

The **essence** is the part in us that contains the universal and the individual gifts of our being. The feeling of joy is an example of a universal gift, and our own musical talent is an example of an individual gift. We can perceive pure and unadulterated essence in an infant.

The basic feeling of essence is: "I want to express myself, give my gifts to the world and be blessed by the world."

The **wounded child** is the stronghold of shame, fear, guilt, self-doubt, etc. Trobe referred to it as "the layer of wounded vulnerability" (Trobe, *Face to Face With Fear* 15). Here reside the unhealed wounds of rejection, humiliation, violence, abuse, shock, etc., both from our parents and family as well as from our childhood environment in general.

The basic feeling here is: "The world is a heartless and unsafe place."

The **protective layer**, created by us, is our strategy to no longer feel what hurts us and to potentially no longer be hurt. The price for this is the partial or total renunciation of vitality, and life itself. We take on roles and wear masks to present to the world. The protective layer in constellations is always the part that cannot feel or doesn't want to feel. With trust-building measures such as mindfulness, clarity and honesty, we may pass through the protective layer.

In contrast to Trobe, in my experience we meet a special guardian of the threshold before we get to the wounded part: **the loyal soldier**. This metaphor is taken from Bill Plotkin's book *Soulcraft: Crossing into the Mysteries of Nature and Psyche*.

The **loyal soldier** is an inner part of our personality that is specifically placed there to watch over the threshold of our wounded part. He isn't someone with whom you can discuss or argue. He has the clear order to not let anyone pass. It is therefore important in constellation work (and even in our inner work, if we want to work with our own vulnerability), to make the inner soldier realize that the war is over. As long as the inner soldier thinks that the old war still prevails, he will not let anyone pass. In a figurative sense, we must provide him with his dismissal papers and appreciate and recognize his efforts. Only then will he give way for us to go into the wounded part. Now you can work with this part and healing can begin.

When we have worked with the wounded child for a while, we have to try to integrate it back into the essence. That is when we get confronted with two new guardians of the threshold: the **Inner Critic** and the **Inner Judge**.

The **Inner Critic**, with the induction of feelings of shame, is trying to prevent the integration of the wounded part into the essence. It is the internalized voice of parents and authority figures of our childhood, which became independent in us. He tells us phrases such as "You are not worth it!", "You are unworthy!", "Who do you think you are, that..." etc.

The **Inner Judge** operates differently. "You are responsible for your mess yourself!", "It's your fault!" etc. He is always causing guilt to rise in us and with that tries to prevent the re-integration of the wounded child.

Both guardians of the threshold need to be addressed with a healthy, clear and mature adult consciousness. Here it is the task of the facilitator to accompany clients and to assist them, where appropriate, when they slide back into the inner child position. This is not an instant path to success, but a gentle, respectful way that has each client check in with their own limits and possibilities repeatedly, until a resolution and healing can be found.

What has the protective layer model to do with happiness in a partnership?

Many mutual misunderstandings and injuries happen when partners meet each other at the level of the protective layer, so that a deep love can't evolve. When we keep our protective layers up during our partnership, we can't build a deeper understanding of our partner nor truly create a lasting bond.

It is therefore important to repeatedly question oneself:

Do I act or communicate solely from my essence or from my protective layer or even from my wounded child? And from which level does my partner relate to me?

Becoming aware of this helps to open the partnership so that it really fits together in love.

It helps to be aware of this in order to open ourselves in love to our partner.

The four basic settings of the Drama Triangle in Transactional Analysis

According to Transactional Analysis, the following are the basic elements in relationships:

I'm OK, you're OK.

I'm not OK, you're not OK.

I'm OK, you're not OK.

I'm not OK, you're OK.

In intimate relationships, all four are found, but the only healthy attitude is the first: I'm OK, you're OK.

The three others lead to unhealthy relationships with dependence patterns and game playing in the Drama Triangle.

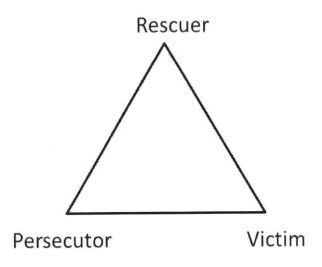

Figure 3: Drama Triangle

The term Drama Triangle, coined by Stephen Karpman, is best explained by an example:

A couple is quarreling on the subway and eventually the man (persecutor) begins to beat his wife (victim). Another passenger (rescuer) gets involved to help the woman by restraining the man. Suddenly the woman shouts at the passenger to leave her husband alone. Now the woman is the rescuer of her husband (victim), who is being restrained by the passenger (persecutor).

This is typical for the drama triangle. The roles of persecutor, victim and rescuer can instantly change and the whole thing takes on the character of a game. However, the attraction of this game is very strong and it is generally accepted in the social context. People seeing themselves as victims of x (where x can be both circumstances and other people) is widespread. Rescuers are celebrated, persecutors are vilified. And the rescuers of today may become the persecutors or victims tomorrow.

In the couple's relationship, it's important that we recognize it early when we get into a drama triangle (or already are in one).

How?

By posing again and again the following questions in conflict situations:

– Do I believe I am the sole victim or persecutor?

– Is the other one like a rescuer for me?

– Do I want to save the other person?

– Do I feel the need to hurt the other or do I long for revenge?

If we answer one of these questions with YES, we must try to internally take a step back and say STOP.

A drama triangle is an endless game with unending role changes. Constructive solutions can never come when in the triangle.

This requires us to have a certain degree of awareness of these mechanisms.

In constellations the drama triangle prevents the way to real solutions. First, the constellation facilitator needs to bring all members involved to think, feel and act like mature adults. Only then are real resolutions possible.

The 5 Love Languages by Gary Chapman

The priest and therapist Gary Chapman published important findings in his series of books *The 5 Love Languages* that integrate well in constellations.

He assumes that every person — usually imprinted by the parental home — has special needs as to how love must be communicated to them.

In his experience there are five channels by which love can be received as nourishing.

The first 'language of love' is compliments. Everyone likes to hear them, but some people actually starve emotionally when they don't get attention through compliments.

As a second language of love Chapman identified helpfulness. To be offered help and to receive supporting acts gives these people the feeling of being loved.

Another language is sharing quality time, togetherness without distractions. This is for people who see that as the real proof of love.

The fourth language of love is showing affection in the form of small or large gifts of any kind. This is not about the material value of the gift, but more about its symbolic content: He/she has thought of me and brought me something.

The final language of love is physical expression through, for example, stroking, caressing, touching and sexual intimacy.

The important point in all these languages is that the couple discovers the language of their partner, and can show their love in a way that fulfills the partner.

Chapman introduced the metaphor of the empty love tank for unfulfilled needs. If over a long period of time either partner is not addressed in his language of love, the love tank empties more and more, resulting in quarrels at first, and finally leading to separation and divorce. No one can remain permanently with unmet needs in a relationship.

When working on a couple's conflict the facilitator then poses this important question in a constellation:

How are you determining that your partner loves you (or doesn't love you)?

If the answer is "He never wants to spend time with me!," we can conclude there is an empty love tank and the need for quality time. The facilitator can bring awareness to the couple by explaining to them the five languages of love.

That should be enough about external input to our observations of family systemic constellation work and happiness in relationships.

What topics I won't touch upon

Relationship problems can have so many causes that it is beyond the scope of this book to dwell on all of them. Therefore, in this work we shall focus only on those causes that can be resolved particularly well through family systemic constellation work.

Through the experience of trauma, it often happens that you can't participate in life fully and thus relationships become difficult. The closeness of a partnership can trigger reactions from a traumatized person in many different ways. Few partners can permanently live with someone who repeatedly shows inexplicable reactions to certain issues.

In my opinion, the resolution of trauma needs specific trauma therapy, which takes time. Apart from the broken movement toward a parent which is a special form of bonding trauma, I won't deal with any other traumas in this book.

The rejection of physical contact due to disgust, phobias or similar phenomena also won't be addressed here — you can resolve this with family systemic constellation work, but that is only one possibility amongst many.

This book can't and won't replace therapy. It's an addition and a preparation for a constellation. A good family constellation facilitator won't leave you alone with the result of a constellation, and usually offers you some kind of further support — but you should demand it as well.

What Happens in a Systemic Family Constellation?

The General Outline:

Interview

Choosing the Representatives

Systemic Constellation

Closing Interview and Review

The Interview

During the interview the facilitator will ask the client or issue-holder for a description of the problem and some background information. Sometimes you'll receive a questionnaire prior to the constellation in order to give you time beforehand to research your family background and events that might be of interest. It can be helpful to contact your relatives who have knowledge of the family history so that you can fill out the questionnaire as well as possible.

The interview helps the facilitator to get relevant information. However, some facilitators might say that they don't need extra information, because all the important aspects and dynamics will appear during the constellation.

Choosing the Representatives

Once the issue is clear and the intention for the constellation is defined, you will be asked to choose the relevant representatives, e.g., father, mother, siblings. The facilitator will prompt you and suggest who needs to be represented in your constellation. Even abstract concepts like freedom or pain, places like your childhood home, or symptoms like excess weight can be part of your constellation. These concepts, objects, and symptoms will be represented by participants and they will be arranged in the same manner as the representatives of the people in your family.

If you are the subject (client or issue-holder) of the constellation, you will take a moment to listen to your intuition before choosing the best participant to represent a person in your family system. Trust your gut feeling when making this choice! You will also choose someone to represent yourself, as you will be in the role of the observer — at least in the beginning. (This could vary according on the setting.)

In the Freiburg method that I have developed, the client stands behind the representative and places their hands on that person while taking a moment to think about the person or aspect being represented.

Then they move him or her slowly to a place that feels right. Usually this is within a circle of chairs and participants that defines the realm of the living; outside that circle is the realm of the dead. (This can be redefined if declared beforehand).

Representatives can decline their role at any time, or pass it on in case it is too much for them.

The Systemic Constellation

Once the client has positioned all representatives in the room, they will all be asked how they are doing and what they are feeling in this position. Only later will they be invited to move freely or be moved by the facilitator to a different place.

It is very interesting to notice that complete strangers can represent a family member so accurately that the client perceives them as very authentic and characteristic in that role. Of course, this happens in different ways: sometimes the representation is highly accurate, and sometimes it may lack a few nuances. Why this is possible and happens is still not explained scientifically. What's important is that it works.

During the process of a constellation, all kinds of different interactions can happen that are aided by the facilitator. For example, 'revealing statements' can be exchanged between representatives, or family members will be moved and grouped differently. Representatives will be invited to follow their impulse to move.

At one point in the constellation the client may possibly take the place of their representative, thus switching from the role of an observer into an active role of experiencing, feeling, and taking action within the constellation. This intensifies the constellation experience and deepens the outcome for the client.

The constellation ends with a resolution picture. At this point, the client may wish to continue with a different constellation on another day, in case the first constellation doesn't yield a complete solution or the need for further inner work becomes apparent.

Closing Interview and Review

After the participants return to their places, the facilitator will summarize the constellation fairly briefly in a closing interview and review. Whatever has occurred in the constellation will be set into context with the intentions and issues that were defined during the initial interview. However, this closing interview can be handled very differently depending on the facilitator. Some facilitators won't say a lot, and support the idea that the experience needs time to be integrated and to settle in. Thus they want to avoid too much talk and discussion. Others like to interpret the constellation and even recommend action steps for the upcoming weeks.

This has been a short explanation of a systemic constellation, as it is practiced in the area of Freiburg im Breisgau, Germany. Systemic constellations vary from facilitator to facilitator. Therefore this description can only serve as a rough overview. There are a few videos on YouTube that can give you a glimpse of constellation work and what to expect.

In the next part of this book I will discuss the topic of relationships.

Note: In all illustrations in this book, the shorter side of the trapezoid indicates the direction the representative is facing.

Resources as a Solid Foundation

Our exercise is called 'Pair Skating.' But we can only do it if each can skate on their own.
From *Paarlaufen* by Ulrich Schaffer

In the context of family constellation work, resources are fountains of strength that we access in order to master the challenges in our lives. In most cases we call upon them unconsciously. You can also build new resources. This is practiced in some forms of therapy, such as psychotherapy.

Resources can be:

– Living or already deceased people (e.g., your compassionate grandmother).

– Abstracts concepts like faith, humor, trust in the universe, nature, etc.

– A beautiful and nourishing experience such as a special holiday which nourishes you still, or the birth of your child that was experienced as highly satisfactory.

– Spiritual beings like angels, shamanic power animals, or ascended masters.

– Places like a pond or a mountain that are a place of power; also intangible places — a spiritual space, a 'meta-space.'

– Natural spaces and landscapes: sea, forest, mountains, prairie...

– Temporal events like Christmas time, spring, the full moon, etc.

– Animals and plants: dogs, horses, cherry tree, oak tree, etc.

– Physical activities: dance, yoga, sports, music, etc.

In the context of relationships, I want to encourage you to discover at least one resource of yours (usually you already use it without realizing you are doing so) that meets some specific criteria:

– It is possible that your resource is not human: Of course, your best friend can be a wonderful resource. But I want to suggest resources where you do not have to rely on others. People are not perfect. When a person acts as a resource, it can easily be overwhelming for them (even if they are already dead).

– The resource should be accessible right here and now, immediately, without having to go anywhere. This eliminates places (except the imaginary meta-space), natural spaces and landscapes, temporal qualities, animals and plants, and physical activities. But it doesn't eliminate the experience or relationship that you have to it. For example, if you can connect well with a particular mountain range from anywhere, then the mountain range can be a resource for you.

Hence, abstract aspects or entities, experiences, and spiritual beings are ideal as resources. Since the latter are a matter of faith, I shall confine myself in this book to referring to experiences and abstracts as resources.

What resources will work well for you within the context of a couple's relationship?

What resources do you need in a partnership?

This brings me back to the final two lines of Schaffer's beautiful poem quoted at the beginning of this chapter:

"Our exercise is called 'Pair Skating.' But we can only do it if each can skate on their own."

In a healthy, functioning relationship the partners help each other, support each other and rely on one another. However, once one

of the partners needs the other, the character of the relationship changes. Now we are
in a dependent relationship with an imbalance of power. The one who needs the other
becomes inferior, the other becomes superi-
or. When both need each other, the power
shifts from one to the other depending on
who needs the other more in that moment.
Characteristic for these relationships are
compromises where everyone gives up
something and some of the needs remain
unfulfilled.

In a healthy relationship, both partners are
free and can at any time leave the relationship without harm. They could, but they
don't do it, because they get their needs met
in abundance. While the compromise lives
within a dependent relationship (one loses,
the other wins, or both lose), a 'free' partnership offers synergies in which both win.
They deliberately search for solutions that
take each other's needs into account and
possibly even meet needs that both partners
hadn't been aware of before (over-delivery).

And thus happiness comes into play. When
1 + 1 doesn't equal 2, but equates to 10,
100 or 1000...

Through self-esteem and synergy the relationship turns into a storehouse of nourish-

ing fulfillment and blissful love, in which dignity, observant respect and mutual understanding reign.

Does that sound too good to be true?

It's possible, but first there is something else to do: You must solve old entanglements, inherited beliefs and destructive patterns with the help of family systemic constellation work.

And here we come back to your resources. If you know your resources, you can go step by step on the way to a fulfilling relationship without getting into dependency patterns — not even needing a family constellation facilitator. Resource work is the first step to freedom.

The Resource Constellation

The resource constellation aims to find at least one reliable resource, which then can be worked with repeatedly, or which the client can connect with quickly in a crisis in order to be capable of taking appropriate action.

Case 1: Anastasia

Anastasia is Russian-German from Uzbekistan who came to Germany 15 years ago. She frequently has gotten into co-dependency relationships. Before looking at that issue specifically in a later constellation, Anastasia decided to have a resource constellation in order to strengthen her ego force.

In our lengthy interview we honed in on four resources:

R1: her Orthodox faith

R2: her first riding lesson

R3: music by Rachmaninov

R4: nature

We constellate. Anastasia selects a male representative for her faith and the music, and a female representative for riding lessons and nature (she also chooses a woman to represent herself).

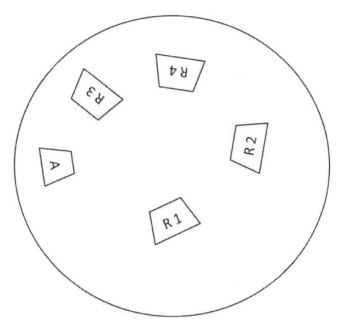

Figure 4: Starting Picture

(A = Anastasia, R1 = Orthodox faith, R2 = first riding lesson, R3 = Music of Rachmaninov, R4 = nature)

It is striking that Anastasia has placed her own representative at the edge and spread her resources widely in the room. I ask her to very slowly step into the middle of the circle, and report back how she feels.

L = Constellation Facilitator; other abbreviations see above

A: (walks slowly to the middle) "I feel watched, especially from faith. Somehow I am not allowed to be in the center... It feels good to walk towards the riding lesson, it warms my heart (by now she has arrived in the middle).

L: Look to faith - how do you feel when you look at him?

A: Small, somewhat uncomfortable...

L (to Anastasia's faith): What do you feel towards Anastasia?

R1: Nothing special.

L: Anastasia, do you agree that faith is not a real resource and we can take him out?

A: Yes, now I see it, too.

Faith (R1) leaves the constellation.

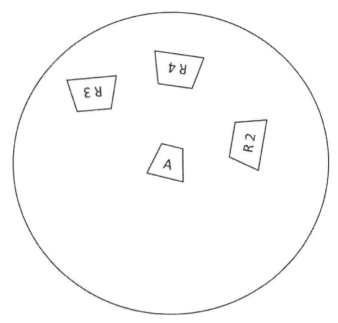

Figure 5: Intermediate Picture 1
(A = Anastasia, R2 = First riding lesson, R3 = Music of Rachmaninov, R4 = Nature)

L: What does her first riding lesson feel towards Anastasia?

R2: Feels good. I look forward to meeting you.

L: How are you doing with the riding lesson?

A (smiling): Very good. May I go to her?

L: Yes, but please walk slowly to her.

She does so, and steps to the right side of the riding lesson. Shortly thereafter, they take each other's hands.

L: What do you feel now?

A: A bond, power, something like 'I can achieve anything.'

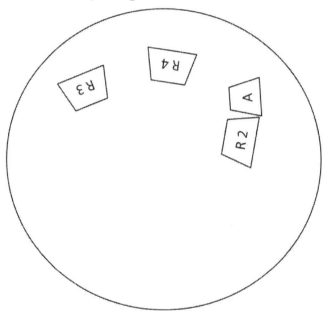

Figure 6: Intermediate Picture 2

(A = Anastasia, R2 = First riding lesson, R3 = Music of Rachmaninov, R4 = Nature)

L: What do you feel about the music, Anastasia?

A: I think it's a pity that it doesn't look at me. I would also like to go to her.

L (to R3/music): What's with you? How do you feel towards Anastasia?

R3: Good, but I'm a bit absent-minded and keep looking into the distance.

L (about R3): Can you look at her?

R3 (turns to A): Yes, but it's not easy.

L (to Client Anastasia): Did anyone else in your family like to listen to Rachmaninov?

A (Client): Yes, my father. I liked to sit on his lap while he listened to a vinyl record when I was very young.

L: That's something very beautiful. But we don't want to use people as a resource. And the music has more the character of the relationship with your father, in which you were naturally dependent as a child — that doesn't quite fit into our constellation intention. Can you see that?

A (Client): Yes. I wasn't really aware of that when I chose the music of Rachmaninov.

L: Well, then we can take the music out of the constellation, if you agree.

A (Client): Yes!

R3 leaves the constellation, and sits down.

L (to A's representative): How do you feel when you look at nature?

A: Good. She seems very calm and deliberate.

L: (to R4/nature): What do you feel towards Anastasia?

R4: Openness. She is welcome.

L (to A's representative): Take your place next to nature.

Anastasia steps to the left side of R4/nature.

L (to A's representative): How are you feeling?

A: Here and grounded. I can feel a subtle but powerful force coming from nature. That feels good.

L: Would you like to stand so that you have nature at your back?

A: Yes, gladly.

L: And?

A: Very pleasant.

L (to R2/riding lesson): Come next to Anastasia, please.

R2 steps next to A, R4/nature behind them.

L: Keep that arrangement and move with Anastasia into the middle.

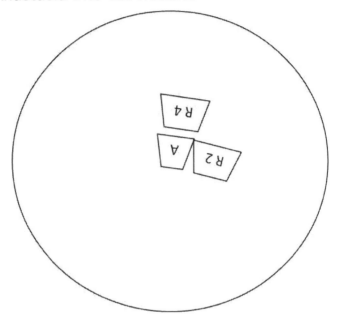

Figure 7: Resolution Picture

(A=Anastasia, R2 = First Riding Lesson, R4 = Nature)

Anastasia steps into the constellation herself and takes the place of her representative.

L: How are you doing here with your two resources?

A: Super! (standing tall) I feel like I have grown 2 inches.

L: Take a moment and feel into it a bit. Then we will finish the constellation.

In this constellation we were able to confirm two resources for Anastasia. Both are powerful and she can connect with them in her mind and with her heart any time.

The other two resources turned out to be unsuitable (music) or only socially desirable (faith). Sometimes we believe that something is a resource because it is recognized as a general source of energy. However, resources are highly individual and don't care what others think about them. This is why the resource validation is so important in a constellation.

Sometimes resources are also context-dependent. In a constellation about a woman suffering abuse, I would always be careful with a resource that is represented by a male representative. It might not fit into that particular case, but it could be THE resource in another instance.

Separating in a Healthy Way from Ex-Partners

We are all people with a more or less long history when it comes to relationships. And in the past a relationship has probably ended in a separation at least once. The breakup was probably painful, and depending on the circumstances which led to the separation, perhaps ugly.

From the perspective of family constellations many separations haven't been carried out correctly, so that there is still something left over from the old relationship. This then affects and interferes with a new relationship, preventing us from living in the best way with the new partner. For example, one might only be about 90% committed to the new relationship, while 10% of you is still tied to the old one, waiting to be released.

Family Systemic Constellation Work has developed rituals and phrases of resolution that are designed to effectively dissolve an old relationship for all parties involved. This is especially important when children are affected by the separation, since your relationship to your child as a parent still persists.

Case 2: Paula

Paula has been with her boyfriend Dieter for two years. The two often have arguments based on jealousy. Dieter accuses her that she still has contact with her ex-boyfriend Marek, who had left Paula for another woman. Although by now she has accepted his leaving, her pride is still injured. Also, Marek is the kind of guy who likes to keep several women in the background at the same time. Paula can perceive that too, and asks to finally disconnect her bond to Marek with a constellation. Marek is of course not open to that, and so Paula constellates on her own. She wants to finally enter into a deep relationship with Dieter.

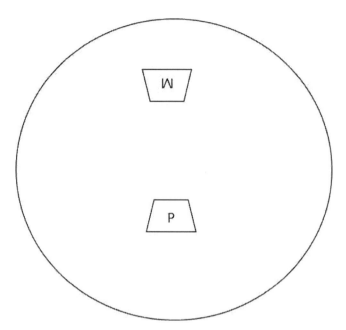

Figure 8: Starting Picture

(P = Paula, M = Marek/ex-boyfriend)

Paula places the representative for herself and the one for Marek exactly across from each other. The two look at each other, and Marek smiles.

L = Constellation Facilitator, P = Paula, M = Marek, MF = Marek's girlfriend, OW = other woman

L (to P): How are you doing with Marek?

P: Well, almost too well. My heart is beating faster.

L: Do you still feel love for him?

P: Yes!

L (to Paula): Do you feel the same as your representative?

Paula: I don't know... Not consciously.

L: Well then, we'll see.

L (to M): How are you doing with Paula?

M: Good. I find her attractive.

L: What do you feel towards her?

M: Attraction... desire...

L: Can you feel love for her?

M: Maybe...

L: Maybe?

M: Yes, I can feel my heart beating.

L (to P): How are you doing with Marek's answers?

P (sighs): That's just him...

L (to client Paula): Let's add his current partner!

Paula chooses a representative and sets her up in the constellation:

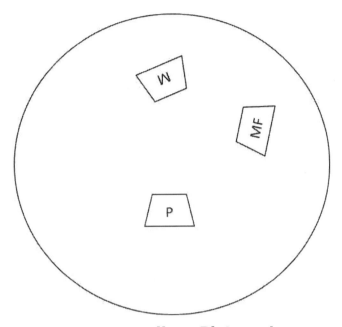

Figure 9: Intermediate Picture 1

(P = Paula, M = Marek/ex-boyfriend, MF = Marek's girlfriend)

L (to M): How are you doing with your new girlfriend?

M: Good. I find her very attractive.

L: Do you love her?

M (hesitates): I think so...

L (for MF): How are you doing with Marek?

MF: Wonderful. He is great...

L: How do you feel about the fact that he thinks he loves you?

MF: Oh, men can't express their feelings very well. He loves me ...

L (to client Paula): Please set up another attractive woman who is interested in Marek!

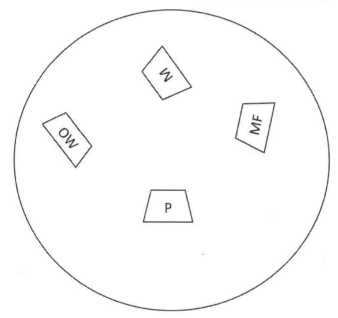

Figure 10: Intermediate Picture 2

(Paula, M = Marek/ex-boyfriend, MF = Marek's girlfriend, OW = Other Woman)

L (to M): How do you feel about the new woman?

M: Good. She looks interesting.

L (to OW): How are you doing with Marek?

OW: Good. He's probably a good lover, but after that I better leave quickly..

L (to P): How are you feeling about what you've seen so far?

P: I'm jealous.

L: Of what?

P: The two women.

L: And Marek?

P: He can't help it... I mean...

L: Who again left whom?

P: He left me...

L: What do you feel now, now that you look at Marek?

P: I'm hurt.

L: Anything else?

P: Mmm... I'm actually quite mad at him.

L (to OW and MF): You can now step out of your representations again. Come into the constellation yourself, Paula — if that's OK by you.

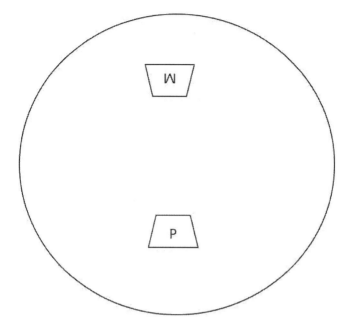

Figure 11: Intermediate Picture 3

(P= Paula, M = Marek/ex-boyfriend)

Paula steps into her representative's place in her constellation. During a longer process, Paula expresses her pain and anger towards Marek. Marek remains relatively unimpressed by all that, and waits out her ranting.

L (to P): It doesn't look like Marek is open to joining the separation ritual. I will now give you some sentences that are part of the ritual. You can imagine that Marek's soul perceives it and participates, even if he doesn't play along here. You can rephrase the words as you see fit.

"Marek, for what didn't work between us, I take my share of the responsibility. I leave your share with you."

P: Marek, for what went crappy between us, I take my share of the responsibility. I leave your share with you!

L: I thank you for the positive things that you have given me. I take them with me into my future.

P: I thank you for all the great, beautiful and good moments that you have given me. I take them with me into my future.

L: I give you a big place in my heart, and let you go on with your life.

P: I give you a big, big place in my heart, and let you go on with your life.

L: Now choose a representative for Dieter and set him up.

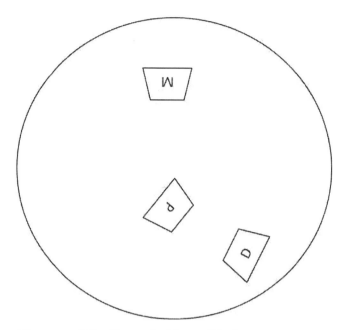

Figure 12: Resolution Picture

(P = Paula, M = Marek/ex-boyfriend, D = Dieter/current boyfriend)

L: Can you tell Dieter: "Now I'm here for you"?

P: Yes (smiling) — Now I'm here for you!

They embrace. We bring the constellation to a close.

Since in this constellation the ex-boyfriend wasn't present and also his representative didn't cooperate, the separation was executed in this case only from one side — which in general is fully sufficient. Of course, it would have been desirable, and also would have been very beneficial to Marek, if the ex-boyfriend had been able to set her free as well. However, in constellation work we don't intervene or interfere in other's destinies without permission. Marek has his own issues to work on.

Paula is now entirely free of Dieter. This is, of course, no guarantee that the relationship will last forever, but the chances for a happy relationship have increased considerably by letting go of the old.

That a constellation can take a different turn is shown by the constellation of Wolfgang and Vera.

Case 3: Wolfgang and Vera

Wolfgang had contacted me through my website and asked if he could see me with his ex-wife. Later we talk on the phone. They separated a year ago and share the care of their 6-year old son. Vera is willing to come to a constellation. Both of them have new partners by now. Nevertheless, they get into fights over how to parent Dennis, their son. Wolfgang thinks there is something unfinished, because he thinks the fights are out of proportion to the issues they are discussing. He asked Vera for a constellation for themselves and also for Dennis' benefit.

Each of them chooses a representative and sets them up across from each other.

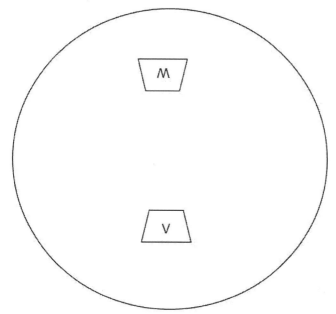

Figure 13: Starting Picture

(W = Wolfgang, V = Vera)

Both representatives still feel love for each other — apart from other feelings like frustration and hurt.

I ask Wolfgang and Vera to step into the constellation themselves.

L = Constellation Facilitator, W = Wolfgang, V = Vera

L (to both): In addition to the negative feelings that should be expressed in a separation ritual, there is also sometimes love that was restrained by something. You have the opportunity to express this love and to let it flow here and now. Does anyone want to say something?

W (to V): Yes, I'll start: Vera, I'm sorry that I couldn't show you my love as you had needed it. I am sometimes still very sad about that.

V: I... feel the same. I always had hoped that we could improve our communication with each other over time... and... then it was over.

W: A part of me still loves you...

V: I know — I never doubted your love. But living with you was no bed of roses...

L: Stay with the unspoken love and don't go into the accusations — we can do that later.

W: OK. (to V): Do you still have love for me in your heart?

V: Yes. A part of me still loves you. But I love Thomas now too and want to start over with him.

W: I understand that. I love Ute.

L: Now, don't focus too much on the new partner. Do you notice how you dodge the feeling of love for each other?

I slowly guide them both through the painful process, and by the end the unspoken and restrained love can finally flow — with the final regret that it didn't work out for them.

Both are very touched. Then I add a representative for Thomas and a representative for Ute into the constellation in order to bring it back to reality.

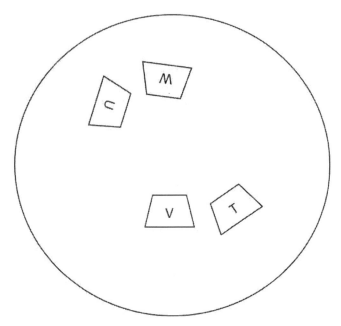

Figure 14: Intermediate Picture

(W = Wolfgang, V =Vera, T = Thomas, U = Ute)

L: In reality, it looks like this. Both of you feel towards your new partners. How are you doing with Ute, Wolfgang?

W: Good. I am very happy with her.

L: How are you doing with Thomas, Vera?

V: Good as well. I love him.

L: You don't want to get together with each other again?

W & V (almost simultaneously): No.

L: Is there something that still needs to be clarified? Or are you ready for the separation ritual?

W & V (again almost simultaneously): No. Yes.

The representatives of Thomas and Ute sit down again.

L: Assume a comfortable distance from each other that makes both of you feel at ease.

They try something and then stand a little closer than at the beginning of the constellation:

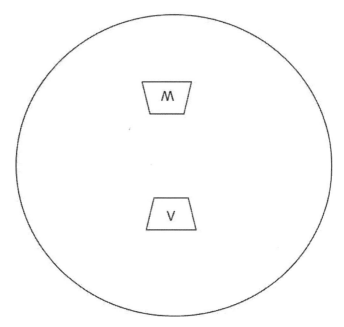

Figure 15: Resolution Picture

(W = Wolfgang, V = Vera)

I then offer them the sentences of the separation ritual (not shown in the dialog).

W: Vera, I thank you for all the good that you have given me. I take it with me into my future.

V: I, too, thank you for all the good that you have given me. I take it with me into my future.

W: Vera, for what went wrong between us, I take my share of the responsibility. I leave yours with you!

V: Wolfgang, for what went wrong between us, I take my share of the responsibility. I leave yours with you!

W: I give you now a big place in my heart and let you go on with your life. As parents though, we remain united for the sake of Dennis.

V: I give you now a big place in my heart and let you go on with your life. As parents though, we remain united for the sake of Dennis.

This concludes the constellation. Unfortunately it doesn't happen too often that both partners are willing to participate in a separation ritual. It would be a good thing for every separated couple to do.

Home Exercise

You can try to perform the separation ritual by yourself at home. It is more powerful in a constellation. But in a longer line of partnerships you can resolve the 'less important' ones at home, and the most important ones in a constellation.

The sentences are the same as above.

* Take a picture or a symbol of the former partner.

* Light a candle next to it in order to enhance your focus and concentrate better.

* Then speak the following sentences while imagining that the soul of your ex-partner responds quietly to them:

> "I thank you for all the good that you have given me. I take it with me into my future."

* Pause. Let it settle in. You may want to look at the flame of the candle.

> "[Insert name], for what went wrong between us, I take my share of the responsibility. I leave your part with you."

* Pause. Let it settle in. You may look at the flame of the candle.

> "I'll now give you a (great) place in my heart and let you go on with your life."

* Pause. Let it settle in. Then blow out the candle as a sign that the separation ritual has been completed.

This also works over long distances or when the spouse or partner is already deceased.

However, if you notice after about a month that the relationship is still not separated, I recommend you arrange for a constellation.

Permanent Conflict as a Sign of an Imbalance of Give and Take

From the systemic point of view, there should always be a balance of give and take. That doesn't have to happen every time, but on the whole there should be this balance. Sincere gratitude from the partner who can't give as much at the moment can also cancel out any imbalance.

Hellinger has coined the systemic statement "The river of life flows forward." This refers to the exception principle mentioned above. Parents give the gift of life which is so much that a child can never compensate for it. As a counter-gesture children offer respect to their parents, and give it forward by having children of their own, or by self-realization and the fact that they enjoy life.

Hellinger recommends that couples reinforce and emphasize the balancing of positive energy, while they reduce and minimize the balancing of negative energy. But in no way should they renounce the balancing of either good or bad. This would have a very destructive effect on the relationship.

He cites the example of a husband's infidelity. If the wife forgave her husband without negative compensation, the man would be indebted to her forever — and he would eventually get tired of that and leave. Therefore, she should do onto him as he has done to her — in a milder version, like flirting with another man. The partner doesn't necessarily need to be aware of this, but the act is definitely a compensation, which is conciliatory, because it doesn't go quite as far and therefore still serves love (any further escalation is moot).

A balance on the positive side can be emphasized by reciprocating a gift, for example, with something even better, and thus increases and deepens the love to each other.

When the balance between give and take in a relationship is on hold for a longer time, the giver will soon feel subliminal-chronic resentment towards the receiver whereas the receiver is drawn away, out of the relationship, because he sees no more chance of recouping the imbalance.

Case 4: Tina

Tina wants to do a constellation because she has been arguing almost daily over the past six months with her longtime boyfriend Dirk.

She holds a diploma in geology and Dirk got to know her while she was completing her studies, as he had just switched his major from chemistry to geology. They moved in with each other fairly quickly, and Tina immediately found a job near the university. Dirk took his time with his second major, and Tina agreed to take on the bigger share of the household costs.

He received his diploma in geology more than a year ago, and was still looking for a job.

Whenever Tina came home, he often was playing PlayStation and she still had to cook and take care of the household, which repeatedly led to friction.

In the end Tina came to the constellation without Dirk.

We begin the constellation with only the two of them.

In the initial setup the representative of Dirk somewhat guiltily avoids the furious glare of Tina's representative.

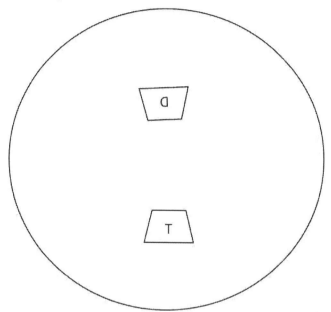

Figure 16: Initial Setup

(T = Tina, D = Dirk)

When asked how she feels, Tina's representative responds:

(T = Tina, D = Dirk, L = Constellation Facilitator)

T: I am angry and feel exploited.

L: OK, feel that, but don't stay with it too long.

I give her emotions some space.

L: Is there something else, perhaps a different feeling?

T: No... I don't know... I would like to shake Dirk.

L: Feel how much it hurts that you only get so little back from Dirk...!

T: I... (she swallows)

L: Yes, what have you swallowed until now?

T: Too... much...

L: Now don't go back into the resentment, stay with your pain, and with how much you have been missing...

T: (crying quietly) I...

L: Can I leave you here, and turn to Dirk?

T: (softly) Yes.

L: How are you?

D: I am ashamed.

L: Why are you ashamed?

D: Because I can't make Tina happy...

L: Mmm, maybe you are taking the easy way out here...

Dirk looks up in surprise.

L: Take your time to really feel how distressing and burdening it is for you that Tina has given you so much and so little came back and comes back from you in return.

D: What...?

L: Try it, feel it...

Dirk is silent and briefly closes his eyes.

L: OK. Look at Tina and tell her: "You can't expect any more from me!"

Dirk is irritated and looks angry and confused at Tina and me.

D: No, that's not true!

L: Good. Do you want to try again to feel how burdening Tina's previous support has been for you?

D: Yes...

I give him space. He looks at Tina, looks away, then looks back at her.

L: What's with you?

D: My shoulders feel heavy and I have a bad conscience.

L (to Tina): That's all I want to do with him. For more he would need to come to a constellation himself.

T: OK...

L: How do you feel when you see him now?

T: I feel sorry for him.

L: Mmm, make a point here by telling him clearly that you can't continue this way.

T: Dirk, we can't continue like this! I want to come to a balanced give-and-take.

Dirk nods in agreement.

L: Take everything of this into your heart. I will say something about it at the end.

We finish the constellation.

As we have seen, there was also pain behind Tina's resentment about the lack of commitment and effort by Dirk. As the constellation has been shown, Dirk is ready to question his current role in their relationship. It would be important for him to do a constellation for himself (but he didn't come). Nevertheless, the two are still a couple today and Dirk has found a job. It can be assumed that the constellation made an impact after all, and it helped Tina to become more conscious so that she could be more clear and assertive with Dirk.

Home Exercise

If you have found yourself in this example, you can prepare for a constellation by posing following questions:

Do you feel an imbalance of giving and taking, of commitment and relationship work in your partnership?

Is there an imbalance from the past that previously couldn't be compensated?

Can you give or take at all? Is giving or taking somewhat difficult or is it easy for you?

Is 'it is more blessed to give than to receive' a motto for you?

Have you ever forgiven a huge misstep of your partner without adequate compensation?

Don't condemn yourself and forget about having socially acceptable feelings! The first step to solving the problem is acknowledging it.

Your honesty with yourself will help you during the constellation to come closer to a beneficial solution for all parties involved.

Relationship Problems due to Binding Love

The bond within a family is a strong force that needs to be reckoned with. Every family member has the birthright to belong in the family system. No one can rise above someone else in order to belong more than others. And no one can deny or refuse the membership. According to Hellinger, the Law of Inclusion applies here. To exclude a family member would create severe consequences for the whole system, and could even lead to the suffering of innocent next generations.

Through binding love we express our closeness and loyalty to our family system. When we are loyal towards the norms and belief systems of our families, we experience an inner joy of greater closeness and belonging to them. This is the 'secret joy of binding love.' In order to experience this repeatedly, we are willing to accept and endure great hardship and suffering.

Ideally, the client realizes that their right to belong doesn't depend on their loyalty to the family's behaviors and beliefs, and that it is safe to just be themselves, no matter what.

In this context, another aspect comes into play.

In his works, the psychoanalyst Carl Jung pointed out that every individual holds a tension between binding love (to one's family of origin) and individuation (personal maturity). In a healthy family system, every individual is given enough room to reach personal maturity without jeopardizing their belonging or being sanctioned by the withdrawal of love.

Unfortunately, this is different in an unhealthy system.

If you are familiar with my book *Stopping the Obesity Pattern With Systemic Constellation Work*, you will see that the following constellation by Sandra is similar Claudia's.

Case 5: Sandra

Sandra is a rather introverted 33-year-old woman. She has been married to Jonathan for five years, and they have known each other for eight years.

She says that they repeatedly clash and have heated fights over nothing, trivial things (in her opinion).

Since Jonathan didn't want to accompany her, she wants to take a look first at what her contribution is to all the bickering.

We start with a constellation that includes Sandra's parents and siblings and Jonathan's family.

This was the initial Revealing Picture:

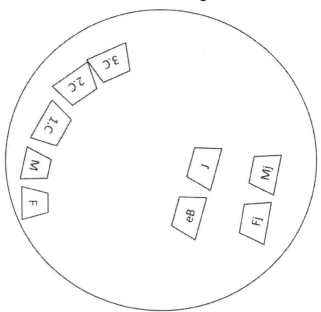

Figure 17: Revealing Picture

(F = Father, M=Mother, 1.C = 1st child = Sandra/client, 2.C = 2nd child (younger sister), 3.C = 3rd child (younger brother), Fj = Father of Jonathan, Mj = Mother of Jonathan, eB = Elder Brother of Jonathan, J =Jonathan)

It's striking that although both family systems are well-organized, Sandra is still in a child position while Jonathan is already in the position of an adult with his parents behind him.

Let's recall the Bible verse: "Therefore a man will leave his father and his mother, and will join with his wife, and they will be one flesh."

This has not yet taken place for Sandra. She is still connected through a strong bond of love to her family system.

It would be ideal if she could face Jonathan and, just like him, have her parents at her back.

One could say that the relationship issues between Sandra and Jonathan are on one hand a problem of individuation (lack of Sandra's maturity), and on the other hand a problem of binding love (Sandra isn't willing to leave her family energetically for her husband).

It is one of the most important, empirical laws of family constellations that the new system must take precedence over the old. Sandra has not yet taken this step and Jonathan did well to point this out by creating conflict in their daily life.

At the same time, the quarrels also point out that the important relationship work, namely the negotiation of new, common values for the new system haven't really taken place. Sandra has simply insisted on her values from her family system. Moreover, she devalued Jonathan's values by calling their quarrels trivial although they were addressing the common values of their relationship.

After I had explained all this to Sandra and she had moved from her child role into the adult role (at the end of the process she placed herself so that her parents were in back of her, just like Jonathan), we set up the fictitious, shared values of Sandra and Jonathan (fictitious because they still have to be negotiated between the two, and there is another important step to be done right now).

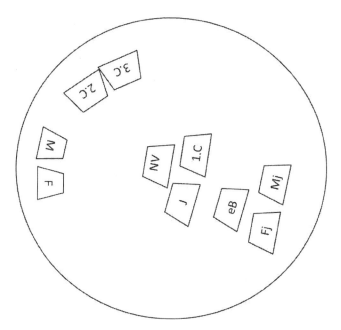

Figure 18: Resolution Picture

(F = Father, M = Mother, 1.C = 1st child = Sandra (client), 2.C = 2nd child = younger sister, 3.C = 3rd child = younger brother, Fj = Father of Jonathan, Mj = Mother of Jonathan , eB = elder brother of Jonathan, J = Jonathan, NV = New Values (of the partners))

I ask Sandra to move as a couple with Jonathan in front of Sandra's family, while the shared values stand in front of the couple. Symbolically both have given energy to the representative of the values. I now ask Sandra herself to come into the constellation.

L = Constellation Facilitator, other abbreviations as above

L (to Sandra): Introduce Jonathan and your shared values to your family, just as if you were presenting strangers to your parents.

S: Hi, this is my husband Jonathan. These are our shared values, which are partially different from your values.

Sandra's parents nod silently, her siblings watch attentively.

L: Tell your parents the following: Please look kindly on me, my husband and our values. If you want, I will happily receive your blessing. '

Sandra says this. However, only the mother is ready to give her blessing. It becomes apparent that Sandra had so far acted out of a kind of anticipatory obedience towards her father.

L (to Sandra): Can you accept the fact that your father doesn't want to give his blessing to you?

S: It makes me sad.

L (to father): What does it do to you when your daughter is sad because you don't want to bless her new union?

F: She knows very well that we have our own principles!

L: Feel into your father's heart. Breathe consciously several times in and out.

He does it.

L: Do you love your daughter?

F: Yes. But the principles are also important.

L: OK. That's your decision. Can you look kindly upon the union despite its different values, and even if you refuse your blessing?

F (hesitates briefly): Yes...

L: Then we'll leave it at that. It probably needs more time, or the participation of a grandson or granddaughter...

We end the installation here.

The rest of the family remains in their positions. But they also don't look unkindly upon Sandra. They can accept that Sandra chooses a different path.

If we realize that we normally can't lose our membership in the family system, we get more room to maneuver freely with our issues at hand. This new freedom needs to be seized.

Sandra did that. It was important for her to leave the safe haven of her family of origin and to engage wholeheartedly with Jonathan. Only then can a deep connection unfold.

Meanwhile, Sandra and Jonathan have two daughters together. They still work on their common values, but their former quarrels have turned into lively discussions in which they address their needs, desires, dreams and goals. This is how a relationship can grow and deepen the love between the partners.

Home Exercise:

Take a blank sheet of paper and something to write with, and retreat to a quiet place where you won't be disturbed.

Contemplate if there are any overt or unspoken beliefs, rules or values in your family system.

What are your partner's values and those of your partner's family?

Write down everything you can think of. These are helpful notes for the preliminary interview to a constellation, and you will realize what conscious or unconscious beliefs currently rule in your family.

Are you ready to break old, unhealthy patterns?

Identification with Another Member in the Family System

This is one of the classic systemic constellations that therapists of other disciplines find almost impossible to solve.

The identification with someone else is a special form of entanglement. In the context of systemic constellation work, an entanglement is due to the fact that we are all more or less strongly involved in the history and destiny of our families. This may mean that we take on burdens for other family members, often subconsciously and without recognizing it. This leads to situations, circumstances, feelings and actions in our lives that we don't want, but almost compulsively encounter again and again.

This may seem unfair and is often evaluated objectively as unfair. But here, the family conscience postulated by Hellinger tries to strike a balance to compensate for imbalances in the system, or at least to uncover inequalities. This can be painful for those affected, but when the signs are interpreted correctly, it can lead to a healing of the family system by uncovering the underlying dynamics.

Entanglements are always accompanied by a weakening of ego strength. After all, you are no longer entirely the master of your own will, which has been repeatedly undermined. This enfeebled ego force will remain weakened until the underlying entanglement is resolved. If they don't resolve the entanglements, therapists will certainly get stuck here.

In terms of relationships, we are interested in the types of entanglement that concern identification issues. They're characterized by the fact that a person unconsciously relives the emotions, traits, lifestyle and behavior, or even the fate of a family member — involuntarily by the client. This leads to self-alienation and a feeling of being controlled by others.

Case 6: Jennifer

Jennifer, age 28, has come to a constellation because of relationship problems with her boyfriend Anton. She has the courage to say that she has problems with her sexuality and that she rarely gets intimate with her boyfriend. She has the feeling that he is about to leave her.

After we were able to rule out abuse and physical impairments, she shares something remarkable.

Sometimes she has a very strong desire for Anton. But when she wants to approach him, she hears a strange inner voice that tells her to stay away.

After she had told us her story, I ask her if there are other family members who have problems with sexuality. She can't think of anyone, but also thinks that no one in their family would speak about that because they are very devout Catholics.

We begin with the constellation of her family of origin. It turns out that in fact there is no particular dynamic. We stop the constellation, and just set up Jennifer, the aversion to sex, and the background of her reluctance to have sex. This was the initial revealing picture:

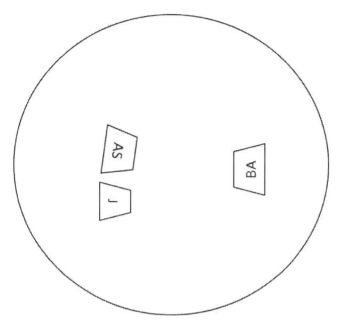

Figure 19: Revealing Picture

(C = Client/Jennifer, AS = Aversion to sex, BA = Background of aversion)

Jennifer's representative is placed very close to the representative of aversion to sex. Both look towards the representative of the background of the aversion. The background of aversion is standing there reverently, and I remember a similar constellation with a Catholic nun (described in my book *Family Constellations and Lack of Abundance*).

I ask Jennifer if a female ancestor had something to do with the church. She considers this for a moment. Then she remembers that the younger sister of her maternal great-grandmother, meaning her great-great-aunt, had been in a convent.

This great-great-aunt's life as a nun, in which a vow of chastity was given, could be the origin of Jennifer's inner voice if she has identified with this aunt. Jennifer feels sym-biotically connected to the aversion.

In the next step of the constellation we re-solve the identification:

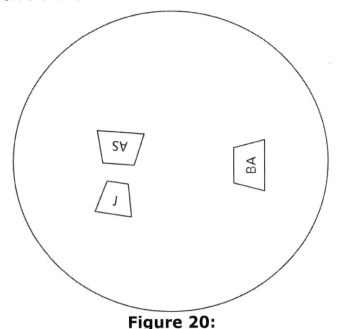

Figure 20:

Intermediate Revealing Picture

(C = Client/Jennifer, AS = Aversion = Great-great aunt, BA = Background of aversion)

L = Constellation Facilitator, GGA = Great-great-aunt, J = Jennifer

L: Look inwardly and feel, Jennifer. Can you perceive yourself as a separate person apart from your great-great aunt?

J: Not really...

L: Try going slowly two steps back... yes, that's good. Feel again... Take your time... tap lightly with your flat hand on your solar plexus several times... How do you feel now?

J: Yes, now I perceive myself as separate.

L: Look to your great-great-aunt — can you easily perceive her as an independent individual, and yourself as an independent person?

J: Yes, now it's quite possible.

L: You are separate and yet you are intimately connected — can you feel that?

J: Yes.

L (to great-great aunt): How is it for you?

GGA: Good, I'm not sure if I entered the monastery entirely of my own free will or whether it was forced by the family...

L: That may well be. But we can only speculate because we are sadly lacking the facts. Can you nevertheless agree that your great-grandniece is innocent and has nothing to do with this?

GGA: Yes.

I take Jennifer into the constellation, as the next steps are best felt and experienced by her (instead of her representative) in order to be effective.

L (to Jennifer): I'll now give you a sentence. You can repeat it the same way or alter it as it best suits you: "You're my great-great-aunt, and I'm Jennifer, your great-grandniece. I respect your fate and leave it with you."

J: You are my dear great-great aunt, and I'm Jennifer, your great-grandniece. I respect your fate and leave it with you.

L: Now choose an object in this room that can symbolize all of your great-great-aunt's acquired burdens/parts/fate, especially the vow of chastity.

Jennifer takes a large white pillow and presses it to her chest.

L: I'll again give you a sentence: "Dear great-great-aunt, this symbol in my hands represents your vow of chastity and other things that I have taken from you. It belongs to you. I have carried it with love for you. Now I give it back. It belongs to you and to your fate."

Jennifer repeats it.

L (to great-great aunt): I will give you a sentence as well: "I respect that you have carried it all for me. It belongs to me and my fate and my dignity."

The great-great-aunt repeats it as well.

L (to Jennifer): Now go slowly towards your great-great-aunt to give her the pillow and then retreat. With every step be mindful of whether you still have feelings that come up or you feel inner resistance.

J: OK...

Jennifer goes slowly toward her great-great-aunt. She can easily give her the pillow and goes back. Then she sheds a few tears.

L: How do you feel now, Jennifer?

J: Relieved. I feel as if I have finally arrived in myself. So completely myself...

L: Take your time and integrate this new feeling fully.

I give her some time. We take a representative of her boyfriend Anton into the constellation.

L: Now turn to a different direction. There is now your new life with Anton, which has just begun.

She walks towards Anton.

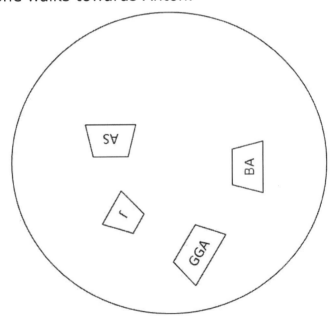

Figure 21: Resolution Picture

(C = Client/Jennifer, AS = Aversion = Great-great aunt, BA = Background of aversion, GGA = Great Great Aunt)

We finish the constellation.

Jennifer can now lead an independent life, without having to repeat the fate of her great-great-aunt and her vow of chastity.

Jennifer wrote me a month later that things are improving and Anton is pleasantly surprised by her increased desire. Nevertheless, she has to get used to listening to her body, which hadn't been present until now due to her great-great-aunt's aversion to the flesh.

She is on a good path to recovery. I recommended that she engage in a lot of body work such as yoga, Pilates, and such, and perhaps in half a year she could take part in a Tantra course together with Anton to arrive completely in her body.

Note: In this example, the client identified with an aunt (a nun) who had taken the vow of chastity. Other identifications could be: a bad-tempered aunt, or a nagging grandma, etc.

There are all kinds of identifications that a constellation facilitator can consider regarding this relatively frequently occurring issue of entanglement.

Home Exercise:

Think to yourself if there are family members who have relationship issues. Make a list with their names.

Do you feel particularly connected to one of them? Are there parallels in your biography and theirs?

When you see this person in your mind's eye, can you perceive yourself as separate from them?

Do you sometimes feel controlled by others, and do you at times have the feeling that you have no real choice?

Let these questions sink in. Your impressions can be important information for the preliminary interview for a constellation.

The Interrupted Movement Towards a Parent

This phenomenon is widespread and can be very destructive. A strong attachment disorder can manifest itself through many symptoms. In this book we are particularly interested in how it influences relationship problems. Although the movement towards either parent or both can be interrupted, a detachment from the mother is seen more often, and in many cases this is more debilitating.

A disconnect can be triggered by the following:

– Circumstances at birth that affected the health of mother or child, and the subsequent measures taken or misfortunes suffered (e.g., being in an incubator, separation of mother and child in the hospital, postpartum depression, not being breast fed or only briefly, death of the mother during childbirth)

– Early death of a parent or parents' divorce, especially during the early childhood years from birth until age 6

– Prolonged hospitalization of the child or a parent, especially during the first four years of the child's life

– Long separations (e.g., a parent is out of the country, the child is given to grandparents or other caregivers)

– War

– Parents who are traumatized, entangled, cold, very strict, or emotionally distant

This rather incomplete list shows how many circumstances can result in a disruption in the child's movement towards a parent.

The following constellation of Angelika was almost identical to the constellation of Dagmar from my book *Stopping The Obesity Pattern With Systemic Constellation Work*.

Case 7: Angelika

Angelika is a 33-year-old who has had only brief relationships for the past several years. She has just found a new boyfriend and now wants to try to break her pattern with a constellation and finally have a long and stable relationship.

In the interview she reports that when she was 3 years old her mother was hospitalized for depression intermittently over the course of several months. Because her father worked, she stayed with her paternal grandmother during this time.

We set up Angelika and her mother only, although it is likely that the movement towards her father was also interrupted.

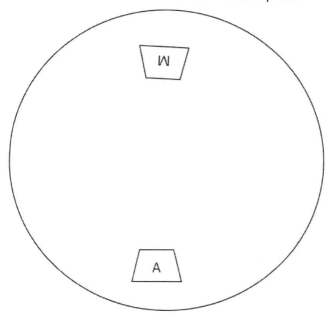

Figure 22: Revealing Picture

(A = Angelika, M = Mother)

The mother looks kindly upon her daughter. I ask the mother to let her daughter come to her and not to move towards her. Angelika's representative is asked to very slowly, step by step, move towards her mother, if she has the impulse to do so. After each step, she should first stop and take in the new position and potential changes she feels.

The first two steps are easy for Angelika's representative. At the third step, she becomes insecure and suddenly feels rejected.

An emotional process rises within her, marked by desire, anger, fear and sadness. Finally she takes another step. After two more steps she turns rigid and can't move, even though she would like to. After no more impulses can be detected, we place her father at her side for support. He, too, looks upon Angelika in a friendly way.

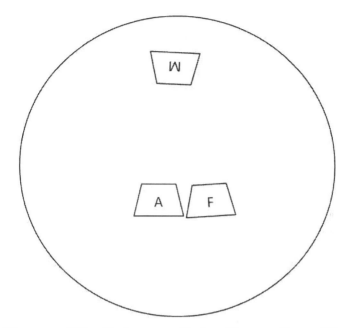

Figure 23: Intermediate Revealing Picture

(A = Angelika, M = Mother, F = Father)

With the support of her father she comes so close that she is only two steps away from her mother. At this important point, we place Angelika herself into the constellation.

I ask the father to move as far away from Angelika as she feels comfortable with. The last two steps she should make on her own in order to integrate the experience better.

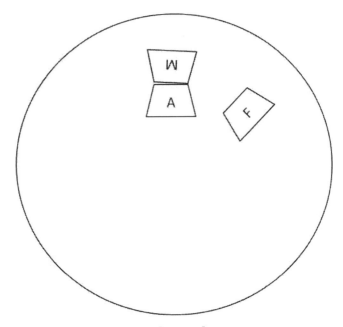

Figure 24: Resolution Picture

(A = Angelika, M = Mother, F = Father)

Finally Angelika is able to sink into her mother's arms, and tears start to flow that have been long overdue. We give Angelika a lot of time to fully take this experience in.

Viewed from the outside this just seems like a person walking towards someone else. But when this process is done mindfully, careful-ly, and by feeling the full range of emotions, then this can be a very transformative and profound experience.

It's very important for the facilitator to constantly pay attention to the energy level, so that the solution isn't influenced by the client overthinking the situation and repressing her emotions.

In this case, the constellation took a total of nearly one and a half hours, including the preliminary interview. It doesn't have to be this long, but it shows what depth the process can achieve if given the appropriate time and space.

Sometimes more than two constellations are required in order to complete the whole process.

Angelika is still with her boyfriend. Moreover, she has been able to build a new, more intimate relationship to her mother.

How important it can be to resolve interrupted movement toward the father can be seen in the next case study with Tobias.

Case 8: Tobias

Tobias is 40 years old, but he did not meet his father until shortly after turning 18, once he had obtained a court order (juristic sentence) against his mother to disclose his father's identity. He grew up as the second of three siblings with his single mother.

His mother always denounced his father, and prevented any attempts to contact him as well as forbidding any relative to ever reveal the father's identity.

So when Tobias met his father for the first time at age 18, he was initially very careful because of his mother's denunciations. Father and son took three years until they came to a reasonably good relationship.

Now Tobias has just met Petra and would like to work on himself to finally be able to have a committed relationship. In fact they have already had quarrels and he wants to discover the true reasons for the unhappiness.

We again do a very simple setup of representatives for the father and Tobias.

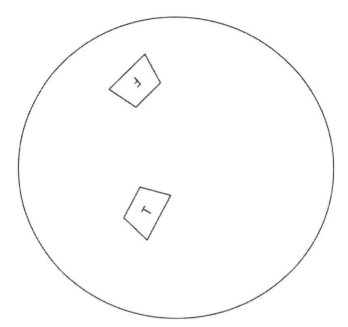

Figure 25: Initial Revealing Picture

(T = Tobias, F = Father)

The representatives of Tobias and his father initially look past each other. Sometimes they look at each other briefly, but then the father averts his gaze relatively quickly.

L = Constellation Facilitator, T = Tobias, F = Father

L: How do you feel, Tobias?

T: Insecure, somehow rejected by my father...

L (to father): Is that so? Does the father reject the son?

F: I don't think so. But he is a stranger to me.

L (to father): Please turn so that you can face him and look at him directly. Can you perceive him as your son?

Tobias and his father turn and are now exactly across from each other.

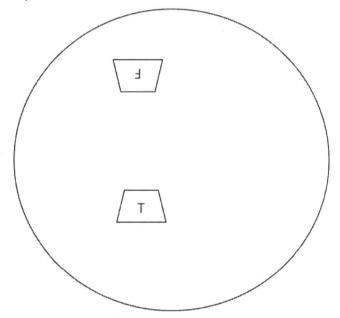

Figure 26: Intermediate Revealing Picture

F: Yes, he's my son.

L: Is he still alien?

F: Yes, but I can get to know him.

L: Tobias, what does that do to you when you hear that your father is open to getting to know you?

T: At first I became angry. Now I'm also sad... I had to fight so long in court until I was allowed to meet him. I had always imagined that I'd be welcomed with open arms.

L: That's OK. It's also the desire of the child within you. Try to step back inwardly and see if you can access your adult ego. Two strangers have met. Your father didn't see you grow up and was kept away from you by your mother. Would you like to give him a chance?

T: Yes.

I then work for a while with Tobias and his mother. He had many derogatory beliefs about his father that he learned from his mother. He is able to return these beliefs to his mother through a ritual, and after that there's a noticeable change in Tobias' mother. The rejection of the father was just another symptom of her rejection of men in general.

Then we continue the constellation with Tobias.

L (to Tobias): How do you feel now when you look at your father?

T: My expectations are doubtful.

L: This is still the aftermath of your loyalty conflict. Look again to your mother.

L (to mother): Can you tell Tobias that he is now allowed to go to his father?

M: Yes. Go to him! My problem with men has only to do with me.

Tobias exhales, relieved.

L (to Tobias): Can you tell him, 'You're the right father for me'?

He repeats it. Now I invite Tobias to join the constellation for the last part.

L: Okay, now please go slowly to him and be mindful at every step whether you can detect any feelings of anger, sadness, angst, shame, etc.

Tobias walks slowly toward his father. At one point anger flares up that we resolve, then shame that we let go of mindfully.

Finally, he stands in front of his father.

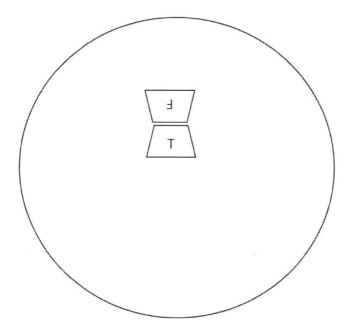

Figure 27: Resolution Picture

L (to Tobias): Close your eyes and go back in your memory to the time when you were a very small boy. Take your time... Open your eyes slowly. Say to your father, "Please...!" And slowly stretch your arms out towards him.

T: Please...!

L (to father): If you have the inclination to do so, take your son gently into your arms.

V: Yes, I would like to.

He takes him gently into his arms. Tobias' body relaxes and he leans his head onto his father's shoulder. Silent tears run down his cheeks.

L: Yes, this is good. Take your time...

After some time we finish the constellation. Tobias' eyes shine blissfully.

Some time later, Tobias tells me that he is still with Petra and things are going well. And the relationship with his father has improved remarkably.

According to my observations, an interrupted movement towards the father creates a lack of masculine energy in the son. Thus he is less attractive to women, which affects his ability to choose a partner. In another constellation we worked on his ancestral lineage of men in order to strengthen his masculine energy.

A "Double Exposure" as a Cause of Relationship Problems

What is a double exposure?

If you see someone else in a person, identify that person as someone different from whom they really are, in terms of family systemic constellation work it is called a double exposure.

This term is borrowed from the field of photography where two levels of reality are captured in one picture by double exposures. The separate images blend together and can't be easily distinguished. In this manner two people become connected. For example, two faces become one face, a person disappears into another, etc.

This is what happens in a double exposure in the context of family constellations: two people who have (almost) nothing to do with each other become blurred together and suddenly one represents the other.

For example, a boss is seen as an authoritarian mother (negative view) or a father sees in his daughter his great love from whom he became separated (positive view). However, both types of views are projections that push aside and ignore the actual person.

Since the real person isn't seen, having been replaced almost entirely by the imaginary projection of another person, relationships get into big trouble. Because no matter what one partner does, the other partner who is making the projection and is trapped by it will interpret every action and every word of the former within the framework of this double exposure. Most of the time a negative view dominates and conflict and disappointments are inevitable.

To resolve the double exposure, the person who is the source of the projection is set up in a constellation. Then the actual (misidentified) person and the person who is doing the projecting are worked with.

Finally, a reconciliation ritual between the original partners concludes the constellation, because the wrongly perceived partner had to suffer under the projection for a long time.

Case 9: Double Exposure — Hilde

Hilde is a quiet woman in her thirties. She wants to do a constellation because she has become stuck in prolonged conflicts again and again with her husband. Mostly their quarrels are about the fact that her husband doesn't help in the household, and that he doesn't take charge when it comes to shared appointments, organizing social events, and staying connected to friends. She feels left alone with these responsibilities.

Hilde feels forced into the role of a home-body and she is rebelling.

During the last fight, her annoyed husband pulled out a list — to her surprise — where he listed in detail his activities in the house-hold and with mutual friends.

Hilde read the list and had to admit that her accusations didn't stand up to an objective review. Nevertheless, they again had a severe dispute over the same reasons a week later.

She fears for her relationship and seeks advice through a family systemic constellation, wanting to find out what is actually going on.

When asked if she knows of a similar situation in her family, she replies after a moment's thought that her parents had at times similar quarrels about these issues.

We initially set up only her and her husband:

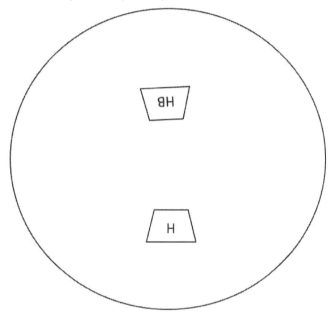

Figure 28: Initial Setup

(H = Hilde, HB = Husband)

The representatives are facing each other confrontationally. The husband is fond of his wife, but visibly annoyed. Hilde folds her arms across her chest and is waiting.

After a few questions and answers the standoff remains unchanged.

Now I place Hilde's father right behind her husband.

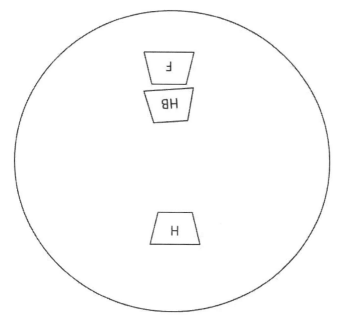

Figure 29: Revealing Picture 1

(H = Hilde, HB = Husband, F = Father), L = Constellation Facilitator

L (to Hilde): Now, listen very carefully to your emotions towards your husband. Look carefully at him and reflect what you feel in connection with him!

Hilde does that and takes her time.

Then I pull her husband out of her sight so that she is looking directly at her father.

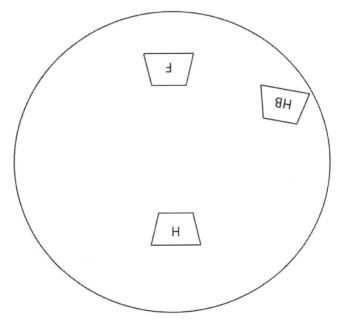

Figure 30: Revealing Picture 2

(H = Hilde, HB = Husband, F = Father)

L (to Hilde): When you now look at your father, do you feel the same things that you felt for your husband?

H: Yes, almost amplified even more!

L (to Hilde): This means that you confuse your husband with your father. We call this double exposure or projection.

I explain briefly what is meant by double exposure. Hilde clearly has an Aha! moment.

She now steps into her place in the constellation.

L (to Hilde): Tell him "You are my father."

H: You are my father.

L (to Hilde): Say to your husband, "You are my husband. I'm sorry that I got you confused with my father."

She says it. The atmosphere in the room becomes very quiet and harmonious.

I place her husband next to Hilde. They hug and then look together at Hilde's father.

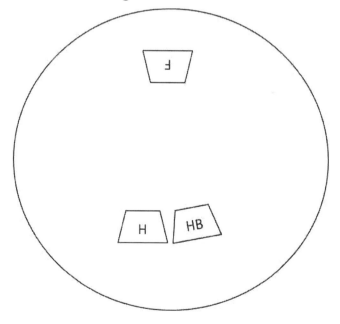

Figure 31: Resolution Picture

(H = Hilde, HB = Husband, F = Father)

I give both of them the space and time to take in the sense of harmony that has been missing for a long time.

Then we finish the constellation.

When Hilde sits down beside me, you can tell that a change has taken place in her. When a projection has been resolved, it takes a moment to adjust to the 'new' world around you. Hilde adjusts surprisingly quickly and well.

Her husband played a significant part in this as his list was a critical eye-opener for her to question her personal perception of him. This comparison with reality led Hilde to come to a constellation. And she did just in time. The confrontational attitude in the initial setup of the constellation already pointed towards a serious threat to the relationship.

As of today, Hilde is still with her husband. Of course they argue from time to time, but never with the intensity and frequency that they did before.

How do I determine whether my relationship problems are related to a double exposure?

If the other person projects onto me:

* I can try what I want, but everything is used against me.

* If I keep a list or statistics, it becomes clear that the allegations are unfounded (reality check).

* I often feel not seen, or falsely perceived.

If I project onto the other:

* Friends and family perceive my partner completely differently.

* Keeping a list or statistics makes it clear to me that the allegations are unfounded (reality check).

* My partner often doesn't feel seen, or feels wrongly received.

This partial list is a first step that you can check if you are affected. It is not about the individual points per se, but the overall feeling you get when you read the list. Does something resonate inside of you?

The double exposure or projection is relatively easy to recognize and to solve in a constellation. Often much more time is needed to resolve a projection when a couple or individual does traditional therapy.

Relationship Problems as a Result of Triangulation

Triangulation is a serious disorder of seniority. It can also be called the Prince (or Princess) Syndrome.

Here we'll confine ourselves to the most important and common triangulation that occurs in a relationship: the involvement of a child in an open or latent conflict between parents. In this case, one parent joins forces with the involved child against the other parent. If it is also an alliance between opposite-sex family members, (father/daughter or mother/son), the child often is invited into and placed in the position of the adult partner.

Generally one can say that a triangulation is a person at a lower hierarchical level being pulled into a conflict at a higher hierarchical level.

Initially that feels terrific for the child, who becomes the confidante, instantly is treated as an adult, and now is someone important! The child also gets a lot of attention — she becomes a princess; he turns into a prince.

The downside is that the child misses being a child and is permanently overburdened by his/her adult role. This also results in competition with the other parent, and in the course of the child's adult life this can lead to problems with same-sex friends and colleagues, and with authority figures. In future relationships, difficulties usually arise because the partner's place is actually occupied by the parent, to whom the inner child stays loyal.

What's interesting in terms of these relationships is that the child gets an abundant amount of attention, becomes accustomed to receiving that, and now expects special attention and treatment in an adult partnership as well.

This then leads to weak and/or brief bonds. But behind this is actually the fact that the partner's place has already been taken by the opposite-sex parent. In particularly severe cases of triangulation the client doesn't even begin to have any relationships as long as the parent with whom they are enmeshed is still alive.

In this context, at times in a constellation we find that two triangulated partners have formed a partnership. This connection is remarkably stable, considering that both are not really in the relationship.

In effect, this relationship becomes a huge screen for any projection, where the daughter seeks her father in her husband, and the son is looking for his mother in his wife.

The difficulty here is that it feels particularly wonderful to be triangulated.

These quite pleasant feelings on the surface are very unhealthy when seen from a psychological point of view. Giving up these feelings is like being expelled from Paradise. Ultimately, a high level of suffering like permanent dissatisfaction or repeatedly failing relationships is necessary before the person is really ready to change something.

From a systemic point of view the triangulated child is missing the strengthening power (as well as the role model) of the same-sex parent, and part of the individuation experience (because the child was directly catapulted onto an adult plane without having a chance to sufficiently develop into it). Furthermore, the child faces a conflict of loyalties because it loves both parents equally, but was forced to deny love to one (and thus displace these feelings into the subconscious).

Case 10: Astrid

Astrid is 42 years old. She has come to the constellation because she finally wants to have a long-term partnership. Again and again her relationships have failed within two years without a clear and discernible pattern. She has a sister who is three years younger.

We place her and a suitable partner in the constellation:

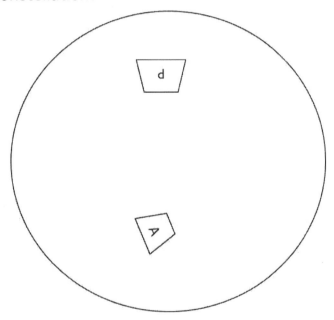

Figure 32: Initial Setup

(A = Astrid, P = Suitable Partner)

Although the partner looks with great inter-est at her, she ignores him and looks away to the right.

We now add representatives for her father and mother.

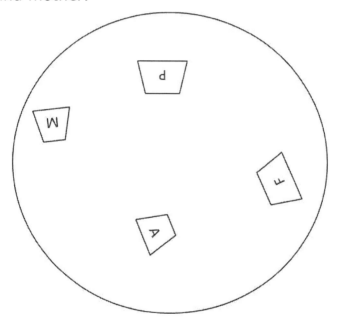

Figure 33: Revealing Image 1

(A = Astrid, P = Suitable Partner, F = Fa-ther, M = Mother)

Astrid beams at her father and he looks happily at her. The mother stands on the sidelines in a somewhat listless manner.

L = constellation facilitator, A = Astrid, P = Suitable Partner, F = Father, M = Mother

L (to Astrid): Do you feel like a daughter towards your father?

A (hesitantly): I don't know... No!

L (the father): How is it with you? Do you feel like a father towards Astrid?

F: No. She seems like a lover or something.

L: Astrid, turn towards your mother. Do you feel like a daughter with her?

A: Somewhat. I feel ambivalent towards her.

L (to mother): Do you feel like a mother towards Astrid?

M: No. She seems to me like a rival.

I let father and mother have some time to reflect on this.

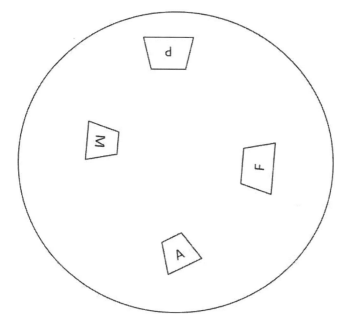

Figure 34: Revealing Picture 2

(A = Astrid, P = Suitable Partner, F = Father, M = Mother)

L (to mother): Together with your husband do you feel like the parents of Astrid?

M: Um... I don't know exactly.

L: It is a biological fact: You and your husband have a daughter named Astrid and she is here to your right!

The mother looks at Astrid slightly puzzled.

M: Yes, probably, it seems to be so.

L (to Astrid): Tell your mother, "Mom, I'm your daughter Astrid. This is my father, your husband."

Astrid says it. The mother's facial expression softens.

M: Yes, this is so.

L (to Astrid): Say something like that to your father.

A: Dad, I'm your daughter Astrid. This is my mother, Mama, your wife.

F: Mmm... I don't see you as my daughter.

L (to Astrid): Repeat it again for your father in other words.

A: Please, Dad, recognize me as your daughter!

F: I'm sorry. I don't feel that way.

L (to Astrid): Try going to your mother.

I ask Astrid herself to step into her place in the constellation. In a longer process she comes to a reconciliation with her mother. I ask her to stand next to her mother and to look at her father.

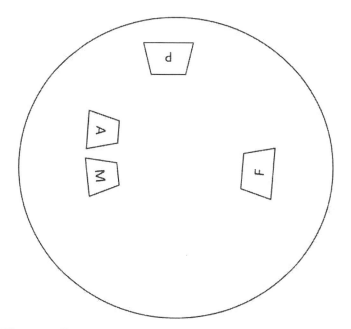

Figure 35: Revealing Image 3

(A = Astrid, P = Suitable Partner, F = Father, M = Mother)

L (to Astrid): Here is a safe place for you under the protection of your mother. Try to feel the closeness and intimacy with your mother.

L: Say it again from here, "Please, Papa, I'm just your daughter!"

She says it. The father doesn't respond.

L: You can't do anything here. Your father has his own issues here. I would advise you

to put up some clear boundaries for him —
do you want that?

A (hesitantly) Yes...

L: If you really want that, imagine now a figure eight lying horizontally. You are standing in one circle of the eight and your father is in the other circle. Keep this in mind. Can you visualize it?

A: Yes.

L: Good. Now think of the eight as we turn to your potential partner.

In the following process, Astrid slowly approaches her potential partner. Now she experiences a genuine interest, and they eventually embrace.

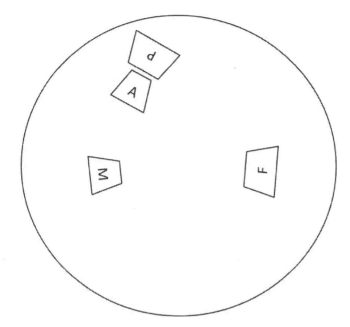

Figure 36: Resolution Picture

(A = Astrid, P = Suitable Partner, F = Father, M = Mother)

Astrid is now open to having a deep relationship. Her father doesn't really want to let go of her, which is why it's important for her to distance herself from him. The fact that she was able to resolve the rivalry with her mother means she now has the power of the female ancestor available, which enhances her radiance as a woman. With this she is of course much more attractive to men who are looking for a committed partnership.

However, it still takes another year until Astrid finds Mr. Right. But if you have been waiting for a long time, another year isn't that much of a problem. It may take a bit longer, of course, if you were triangulated as long as Astrid was.

Case 11: Murat

I have already described the Murat case from the viewpoint of lack of money in my book *Family Constellations and the Lack of Money*. Although he came with questions around his relationship to money, his partnership problems were resolved in this constellation as well. His constellation is almost a textbook case.

Murat is 35 years old and seems like a very cheerful guy with a nice tan, a well-groomed appearance and a winning smile. He says that he constantly suffers from a lack of money, and he wants to finally get rid of that with a constellation. He is the eldest son of four, and has two younger brothers and a sister. When he was 9 years old, his Turkish-born parents got divorced. He broke off three apprenticeships and vocational trainings, and now works in the warehouse of a freight forwarding agency.

We now arranged him and his parents in the constellation circle. The initial setup immediately shows us a triangulation.

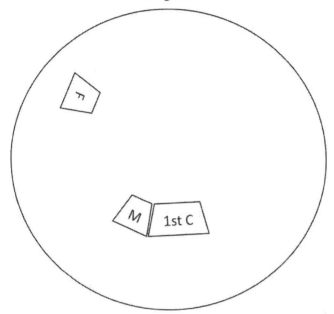

Figure 37: Revealing Dynamic

(F = Father, M = Mother, 1.C = 1st Child/Murat)

Murat is standing on his mother's partner side. His father stands on the sidelines. I ask the representatives of Murat and his mother to look at each other.

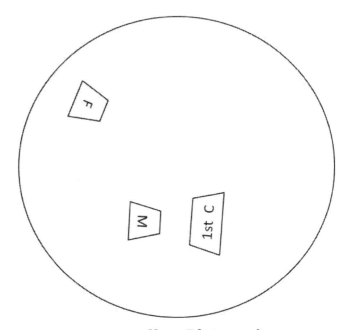

Figure 38: Revealing Picture 1

(F = Father, M = Mother, 1.C = 1st Child/Murat)

L = constellation facilitator, F = Father, M = Mother, C = Client/Murat

L (to mother): Do you feel like a mother to your son?

M: (hesitantly) No.

L (to Murat): Do you feel like a son to your mother?

C: (clear, immediate response): No!

I let Murat approach his father with a bit of distance between them.

L (to father): Do you feel like a father to-wards Murat?

F: Yes.

L (to Murat): Do you feel like a son towards your father?

C: Hmm, yes, yes, but I also have competi-tive feelings.

Next, I have his father and his mother meet. They stand irreconcilably across from each other. I draw attention to their role as par-ents and ask them to say the following:

F (to mother): No matter what happened be-tween us, I'm still the father of Murat, and thus in my role as a parent I remain con-nected with you for the benefit of our son.

M (nods agreement): No matter what hap-pened between us, I'm still the mother of Murat, and thus in my role as a parent I re-main connected with you for the benefit of our son.

I place them next to each other a slight dis-tance apart, and across from Murat.

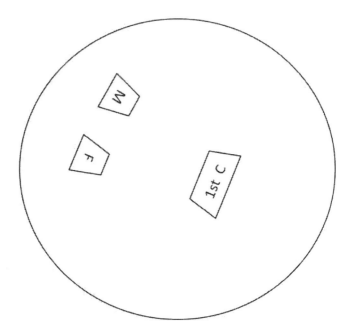

Figure 39: Revealing Picture 2

(F = Father, M = Mother, 1.C = 1st Child/Murat)

You can tell that Murat's mother has become aware of her mother role through the encounter with the father.

I then ask them to say this:

M (to Murat): No matter what has happened between us, this is none of your business. This is a matter between me and your father. I'm sorry that I drew you into this. I am the elder and you're only the youth. I am the mother and you are only the child.

C (to mother): What's between you is of no concern to me. I'm only your son, you're my mother. You are the elder and I am only the youth.

At this point I invite Murat himself into the constellation. The representative had omitted the word 'only' in his last sentence (... and I am only the youth) although I had given that to him.

That was not an oversight, but an expression of resistance against being less important. At this point it's best to work directly with the client.

Even Murat has difficulty saying the word 'only.'

I explain to him what the triangulation shows and how it affects him, and leave it up to him as to how he wants to continue.

I suggest to him a method that the constellation facilitator Wolfgang Bracht sometimes uses to clarify the situation. He is asked to stand on a chair.

Murat is willing to try this experiment.

I let him get a sense of how he feels on top of the chair and in comparison without it. We do this twice to feel the difference clearly.

C (standing on the chair): I feel superior to my father and consider myself the better match for my mother.

C (standing on the floor): Here I feel less superior. At the same time my shoulders are more relaxed.

L: Do you want to try saying the predefined sentences again?

C: Yes!

This time he can say his sentences using the word 'only' without resistance.

Over an extended period I let him move closer to his parents, so that he has enough time to slowly integrate this new situation.

We arrive at the following resolution picture:

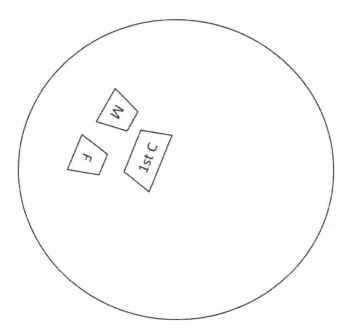

Figure 40: Resolution Picture

(F = Father, M = Mother, 1.C = 1st Child/Murat)

After a long time Murat meets his parents simply as their son. That signifies the loss of a special status, but also shows the relief he feels towards his mother as well as his father, whom he no longer has to compete against.

We leave the installation here. I arrange with Murat to allow some time for the constellation to settle and integrate, and ask him to give me a call after four weeks.

When we finally talk, he tells me that he has gotten somewhat closer to his father, and that he also has a new girlfriend.

We continued our calls, since back then he had meant to get rid of his money problems. In fact, he started taking evening classes and finished his high school diploma, and his financial situation improved visibly.

The girlfriend is now his wife, and they have a daughter together.

How do I know that my relationship problems are based on a triangulation?

The eldest daughter and the eldest son are particularly prone to be affected by a triangulation.

One feels like a prince or princess due to the attention by the opposite-sex parent, with whom one is allied.

Relationships are often short-lived.

In my opinion, a triangulation can only be resolved successfully in a constellation. The most important thing is to first suspect that the relationship problems are connected to a triangulation.

Longing for the Soulmate

"Somebody tell me why I'm on my own
If there's a soulmate for everyone..."
Natasha Bedingfield – Soulmate

The longing for the soulmate is a widespread, glorified and idealized feeling that occurs more frequently in women than in men.

Every person wants to be understood. Everyone has the desire to be recognized and loved in their deepest essence.

Let's be honest: Can we ourselves offer this to others, that which we so long to find?

But for some of us this desire is so strong that it leads to problems in the early bonding with a partner, or even prevents it completely.

Let's take a look at Monique and Giovanni:

Case 12: Monique and Giovanni

Monique comes to me for a constellation because she has problems with her partner Giovanni. He can't meet her needs for intimacy.

When asked whether she has encountered this pattern in relationships before, she answers with a frustrated "All the time!"

"What does your ideal partner look like?" I ask her.

"We love each other, merge and become a wonderful unit. It's like a cosmic oneness. I don't need to tell him my desires, because he feels them and then fulfills them. And in turn, I do the same for him..."

Pointedly I ask her: "But we're still talking about a man of flesh and blood, right?"

She turns quiet and is confused; her eyes are filled with sadness.

"Let's start immediately with the constellation, there's something important happening with you right now!"

She chooses representatives for herself and Giovanni:

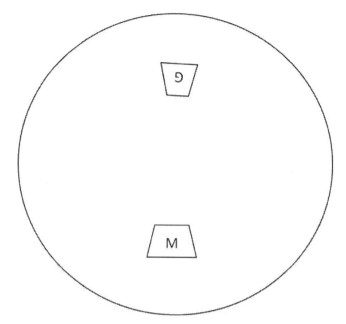

Figure 41: Initial Setup

(M = Monique, G = Giovanni)

The couple is standing opposite each other with a relatively large distance between them. Giovanni seems to be biding his time, but looks with interest at Monique.

Monique alternately looks at Giovanni and at the floor in front of her. In constellations this is usually a sign that someone is looking at a dead person.

I ask Monique if she has lost someone, if anyone near to her had died very young. At first she can't remember anyone. Then she remembers that her mother had once mentioned that while she was pregnant with Monique she might have lost another fetus. So it could be a lost twin who shows up here in the constellation.

I ask Monique to select a representative and then to ask that person to lie down on the floor in front of her.

She chooses a young woman, and places her in the place where her representative's gaze is drawn to her repeatedly.

Nothing changes for Giovanni when the lost twin is added.

But Monique spontaneously goes to her twin and lies down beside her. They look at each other lovingly.

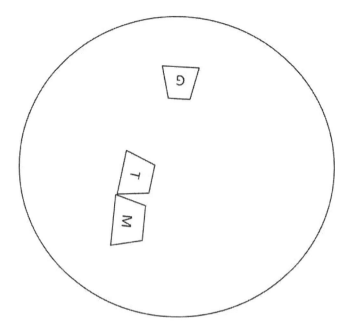

Figure 42: Revealing Picture 1

(M = Monique, G = Giovanni, T = Lost Twin)

The two look at each other for quite a while, and time seems to be forgotten. I give them some room for that.

Finally, I ask Monique to put herself in the constellation so that she can immerse herself in this important experience. I also give her some time for that.

To bring the grief and the pain back into the constellation so that we can arrive at a solution, we decide to trace the date of the miscarriage within the constellation. I ask all the women present to form a circle around Monique with the twin representing a womb.

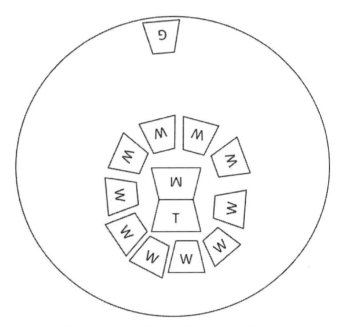

Figure 43: Revealing Picture 2

(M = Monique, G = Giovanni, T = lost twin, W = Women forming the uterus)

The meeting of the twins in the womb becomes even more intense. Monique is beaming with happiness. She and the twin are entwined.

After some time, the twin leaves the symbol-ic womb and also steps out of the circle of chairs.

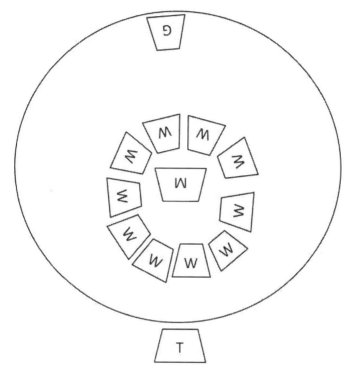

Figure 44: Revealing Picture 3

(M = Monique, G = Giovanni, T = Lost Twin, W = Women forming the uterus)

I ask the twin what was the reason for her leaving.

T: "There was not enough for both of us. One had to go."

That resonated with Monique. During several steps in the constellation Monique was able to say goodbye to her twin, and let her go in peace.

I ask her now to look again at Giovanni and invite each of them to follow their impulse to move.

It is immediately apparent that Monique can now see Giovanni with different eyes. They carefully walk towards each other and touch each others' hands lightly.

Giovanni hugs Monique very gently. The whole process takes some time.

Eventually, I ask the two of them to symbolically look at a white, blank wall that represents the canvas of a new kind of relationship for them from now on.

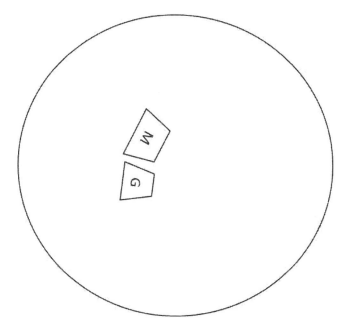

Figure 45: Resolution Picture

(M = Monique, G = Giovanni

They hold each other lovingly by their hands.

Then we end the installation.

Monique had been looking for something in Giovanni that neither he nor any other man would be able to give her: the symbiotic intimacy of her twin sister.

Her longing for a soulmate with all the ideal attributes was a sign of her prenatal trauma, which had been caused by her twin leaving before birth.

After this constellation, she can start with Giovanni once again anew.

Of course, Monique might feel from time to time symbiotic desires. When she notices them she can from now on direct them to the right recipient: her twin sister.

Maybe then she ignites a candle in memory of her and thinks of her fondly.

General statements about the lost twins

The "vanishing twin syndrome" is unfortunately often concealed from expectant mothers by medical professionals. Only after three months when the twins (the multiples) are still vital is the mother informed that she is expecting twins (multiples). The numbers of lost twins vary from 12.5 to 20%; in my training figures between 25 to 30% were reported. So it is quite a frequently occurring event with profound consequences. These episodes are almost always of a traumatic nature and characterize the bonding ability and the bonding behavior.

How do I know if I may have a lost twin?

If you answer yes to most of the following questions, it is very likely that you have lost a twin:

You feel a great longing for a soulmate.

There was some bleeding or discharge involved during you own pregnancy.

The topic of death resonates in you with both yearning as well as terror.

There is an inner feeling that something is missing from you.

You live for two: eat, shop, work, etc.

You have unexplained feelings of guilt, which are not explainable from your autobiography.

You have a strong desire to travel, which has the character of a search.

You are greatly involved in your spiritual quest.

You chose a helping profession.

I want to point out that the phenomenon is rare, but that is precisely why it can be discovered and solved only with family systemic constellation work.

Constellating with a Relationship Being

It can be useful to include a relationship being into a constellation in order to find out how the relationship of a couple is doing in general.

Can the relationship still be saved?

Is there any flow of love at all between the partners? If so, does it flow from both of them?

Are the current problems only distractions from deeper issues?

Does the couple instigate 'games' in order to get intimate, and if so, why?

Do they organize drama because the relationship has become boring?

Do they try to emulate Hollywood love, while ignoring the wonderful husband-wife reality?

Does love prevail on the inside despite heated quarrels on the outside?

The relationship being is a very good indicator of the essence of love between both partners which affects their actions in the relationship as a whole.

In practical terms, both partners jointly choose a representative for the relationship being. The mere selection of this representative can reveal a lot about the state of the couple's relationship:

Can they quickly agree on a representative?

Are there discussions about whether the relationship being is represented by a man or a woman?

Do they choose a younger or older representative for their relationship being?

Finally, the constellation facilitator needs to be sure that the representative is really able to fulfill their role, because their statements and feedback in the constellation will weigh greatly.

Statements that resonate should be given special attention.

Case 13: Jean and Claudine

Jean and Claudine are both in their early 40s. They have been together for more than 12 years. Jean complains that they don't have much sex anymore, while Claudine complains that her partner doesn't want to change (both issues are common in relationships).

I tell them how a constellation with a relationship being works.

After some back and forth they pick a young woman as representative for their relationship being. I check for myself energetically whether this choice suits them, and can't sense a 'no.'

We set up the representatives for Jean and Claudine and the representative acting as the relationship being. First, the representative of Claudine is guided to her place. Then Claudine sets up the relationship being and gives it energy. Now Jean steps in, changes slightly the alignment of the representative and also adds energy (which can also be done simultaneously, e.g., the woman over the left shoulder of the representative and the man over the right shoulder).

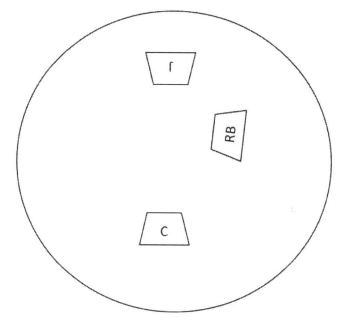

Figure 46: Initial Setup

(J = Jean, C = Claudine, RB = Relationship Being)

Although Jean and Claudine face each other in a relatively confrontational way, the relationship being smiles encouragingly at both of them. It is somewhat closer to Jean and its posture reveals that it is also inclined slightly more towards him.

Claudine bobs up and down a bit annoyed, but is also very attentive. Jean has a slightly dreamy face.

The representative of the two confirms these feelings. So I question the relationship being.

L = constellation facilitator, J = Jean, C = Claudine, RB = relationship beings

L: How is the relationship being doing?

RB: Good. I feel somewhat passed over by Claudine, but I don't feel offended. I am on good terms with Jean.

L: Does love flow between the two?

RB: Yes. Very fine and subtle. No high strung emotions. More like a quiet, leisurely river.

L (to C): Can you relate to the statements of the relationship being?

C: Well, yeah, but that's not the point. He doesn't want to change... at all!

L: Wait a minute, we don't do change management here. This is a partner constellation, in which we primarily address love.

C: Yeah, but...

L: May I invite you to listen to your love...?

C: OK.

L: Look at Jean; look at the relationship being. Right now it's about love. See what you can feel...

(C has ceased to rock on her feet. Her gaze is softer.)

L: Right. Now you can feel it...

C: Yes...

L: Stay with that while I turn to Jean.

L (to J): What's with you?

J: I have a longing.

L: For whom?

J: Claudine!

L: Hmm... How old do you feel right now?

J: What? Uh... I don't know... younger... maybe 30 years old?

L: But you know that you're right now in your early 40s, right?

J: Well, no? ... I mean, I don't feel that way.

L: Look to Claudine, she is 41 years old and you're 42.

J: Yes?

L (and C at the same time): Yes!

J: OK!

L: Jean, it is important for your relationship that you're fully present.

J: Yes.

L (to C): Do that again what you did before, this rocking on your feet that made you seem bigger.

(C does it.)

L (to J): How do you feel when Claudine does that?

J: Small. Not taken seriously.

L (to C): Can you say to Jean "You're an equal partner!"

C: You're... no, it's not true. I feel superior to him.

L: What does the relationship being have to say to that?

RB: When Claudine says that, I retreat. Then I get very tight.

L (to J): How do you feel when you hear that?

J: I'm a little angry and sad.

L: That was said too nicely... Feel into it.

J: OK, I'm pretty pissed. (to C) You're not my mother!

C: Then finally grow up!

J: I am an adult, but I also try to keep our love.

(RB moves closer to J)

L (to J): If you accept too many compromises and lose yourself just to keep the relationship, you will definitely lose Claudine's respect and in the long run lose the relationship.

L: Tell her this: "I stand up as a grown man for me and our relationship!"

(Jean says it.)

L: How does this affect you, Claudine?

C: Good. Sexy. I no longer feel superior.

L: OK. Now follow any impulses to move, but without talking.

C and J move slowly toward each other. The RB smiles. C and J embrace and then spontaneously form a small circle with the RB.

L: I'll leave you here with that.

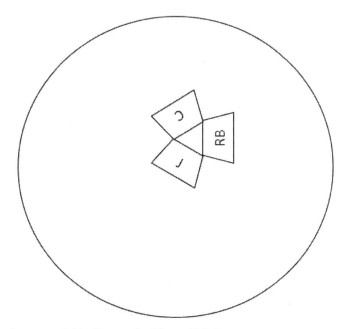

Figure 47: Resolution Picture

(J = Jean, C = Claudine, RB = Relationship Being)

We end the constellation. In the conversation afterwards, I offer them a few observations for the way home.

It became apparent that Claudine had taken on a mother role towards Jean, and she therefore felt superior. Sexual tension always ceases when a wife-husband relationship turns into a mother-son relationship (which Jean detected)

Claudine's effort to change Jean is the ambition of a mother who wants to parent her son — but it is not part of the healthy togetherness of equal partners. Jean's initial, dreamy gaze and his life in the past exacerbated Claudine's mothering, because emotionally she was maturing while he stopped. Here Jean had to first return to the here and now before he was able to step fully into his role as a husband and partner.

The relationship being acted as an indicator of intimacy and distance between the couple as well as a reporter on the flow of love. Although the relationship seemed rather strained from the outside, there was a fine love present between the two, which was a good aid to work with once they both were reminded of it.

That the two chose a relatively young woman for the relationship being could indicate that the relationship still needs to mature further and that it is a bit too female-dominated.

Home Exercise

Imagine in your mind's eye your relationship being:

Would it be more masculine or feminine for you?

How old is it?

Would it stand closer to you or to your partner?

The relationship being is a beautiful metaphor for two people who create something with their love that goes beyond them and becomes its own entity. It has its own existence intrinsically and you can set it up with the necessary respect in a constellation.

Sexuality in the Partner-ship

I almost didn't write this because everything seemed quite clearly presented in the individual chapters, where the connections to sexuality are repeatedly pointed out.

But then I decided to dedicate an entire, albeit brief, chapter to sex.

The prerequisites for both partners having fulfilling sex are, in my opinion, willingness, being at ease, and having some understanding of what sex is and what it means.

Therefore, having sex with animals, children and protected persons (e.g., exploiting the mentally handicapped) is excluded.

Otherwise, everything is permitted, as long as both give their consent — whatever rocks their boat or tickles their fancy, no matter what society, morality or culture may say.

We could close the chapter with this, but let's highlight a few aspects of the previous chapters and put them into some context and order.

Problems During Sex

1. Based on a triangulation

If one or both partners are triangulated, two people meet at different levels while having sex. Most often someone in the father position will meet someone in the daughter position or someone in the mother position will meet someone in the son position.

Certainly this feels wonderfully familiar and is perhaps reminiscent of home. However, the sexual tension is missing in these situations, since a parent position meets with a child position.

Only with the dissolution of the triangulation can sex be experienced in all its diversity.

That's what happened with Heinz and Gerda. Heinz was the classic provider who went to work and brought home the money. Gerda was a housewife and mother. She never learned to be self-sufficient, and from the beginning she was submissive and childlike. Her motto towards Heinz was "Please provide for me!" She had never intended to work. By choosing the child role she automatically pushed Heinz into the parental role.

Gerda discovered that the sex wasn't very fascinating and exciting, and subsequently she had an affair with her personal trainer. Shortly before she decided her marriage was inviable and she was about to get a divorce (and survive with her three kids on Heinz's alimony), Gerda decided to come to a constellation. Here we were able to dissolve and release the triangulation.

Suddenly Gerda saw her husband Heinz with different eyes.

For Heinz, it was a relief to no longer have to be in the father role towards Gerda. He could finally share his secret sexual desires with her. Now the way was clear for fulfilling adult sex and both are still together.

2. Because of a previous great love

If one of the partners hasn't concluded their relationship with an ex-partner, especially when that person had been the great love of their life, sex with a new partner will often not be fulfilling.

This is especially true if the new partner unconsciously realizes that he/she is not really the intended receiver of the partner's love. This can be very hurtful and even block their sexual openness.

That's what happened with Peter and Sieglinde. Peter had had a passionate relationship in his 20s with Judith. When she ended the relationship, his world collapsed. Eventually he got to know Sieglinde, who seemed to be the big prize for Peter.

Unfortunately, she discovered over time that Peter wasn't really present in the relationship — and not during sex. Once he even called out Judith's name during intercourse, which hurt Sieglinde very much.

Only after doing a constellation where Peter actually went through the painful process of releasing Judith did his relationship with Sieglinde improve.

3. Because of the longing for death or injury

Sex is a strong physical expression of vitality/aliveness of every human being. However if a person is strongly attracted by death or has had traumatic experiences, around them one can detect a kind of dampened field that makes real physical and emotional intimacy difficult.

When that type of low energy is present, in particular the sexual relationship suffers greatly. Sometimes it happens that a lot of sex is needed in order to be able to feel at all. But this isn't lovingly passionate, soul-uplifting sex. Rather it's a compulsive attempt to somehow get to the source of life.

Meet Marcus and Miriam. Miriam lost her younger brother when she was a child. Since then, she has felt a certain longing for death. In her relationships she places a particular emphasis on the sexual act. She regularly ended relationships because the men weren't "potent enough" for her.

When we uncovered and released her desire to follow her brother into death during a constellation, she was able to open herself to the other attributes of sex. Now she enjoys fewer but more intense sexual episodes, and she is slowly exploring her sexuality with Marcus.

4. Because of Sexual Abuse

Since sexual abuse is a traumatic experience it has a special place when it comes to sexual activity. It is beyond the scope of this book to deal here with the many shades and its possible solutions.

But I want to offer the victims of sexual abuse some hope. Once they have recovered their self-respect and are able to rediscover sex at their own pace, they can achieve a depth in their sexual experiences that is denied to many others. They have the special opportunity to experience sex as very mindful and respectful lovemaking and thus to override their bad experiences.

5. Due to lack of love

Whoever says that you don't need love for sex is ostensibly right. Basically, sex works even without love. Red light districts around the world sufficiently attest to this.

Nevertheless, this sex is often very poor. This kind of sex usually compensates for loneliness, lack of self-esteem or excessive pride.

The difference in experience is so blatant that it is obvious to most people.

6. Due to an identification

See the relevant sections above.

Good Sex

A provocative headline, I know. I don't pretend to know what good sex means to you. That's the beauty of it, that tastes are different and "to each his own."

But I want to point out that over the long term nurturing, attentive and fulfilling sexuality can only come from the attitude "I'm OK, you're OK!"

This doesn't exclude role playing, BDSM, caviar and champagne, and whatever else is out there, even when the mindset has to be left aside for a moment. BDSM, as an example, is based precisely on the premise that one is OK, the other is not. But in everyday life the equality of both partners must be respected.

The other way round it is very problematic when one partner condemns the other because of their sexual inclinations or interests. Then we are in, "I'm OK, but you are not!"

In addition to the unmet needs of the partner, an unhealthy conflict of rejection is created that sooner or later will blow the relationship apart.

Good sex is connected to being able to share with our partner our most secret sexual desires, without the fear of being condemned, and having at least some hope of getting our desires met.

And thus good sex is also based on transcending one's own limits repeatedly, on experimenting and especially on enjoying oneself in the process.

There is so much pressure to perform in our society, entering our bedrooms with Viagra and the like in recent years. The enjoyment of physical sensations has been pushed into the background.

But the choice is up to us as to whether or not we continue to play this game. Or whether we draw a healthy line and create our own quality sex that is comfortable for us and our partners.

For this, I wish you the courage, the time and the patience to implement this.

Epilogue

Within this book I have shown you a selection of relationship issues and their backgrounds. In my opinion they are especially easily and beneficially solved with family systemic constellation work. Once you have uncovered the true reason for your issue, your relationship will develop into a source of mutual appreciation, respect and deep love.

This takes time, of course, because we tend to fall back into old patterns until we become aware of their effect. After a constellation you can let these old behavior patterns be and with a little attention change the old habits for good.

I am happy for you and wish you a wonderful, fulfilling relationship with love and respect!

From the heart,

Marc Baco

Gratitude

I am grateful for the trust and support of the clients who have provided me with their stories in an anonymous form. I also thank my colleagues in systemic constellation work, who have provided me with matching cases in the context of relationships.

Thanks to Sarah for the cover.

My appreciation to Bert Hellinger for his pioneering work, and I want to thank my teachers Gerhard Walper (Bad Homburg) and Wolfgang Bracht (Freiburg) who have shown me the very different approaches to family systemic constellation work.

Thanks to Laura for the translation and to Sharon for the proof-reading.

Finally, thank you, dear reader, for taking the time to read about this exciting topic.

Recommended Literature

Chapman, Gary. *The 5 Love Languages: The Secret to Love that Lasts*. Chicago: Northfield Publishing (Moody), 2015. Print.

Gray, John. *Men Are from Mars, Women Are from Venus: A Practical Guide for Improving Communication*. New York: HarperCollins, 1993. Print.

Hellinger Sciencia. Spiritual Family Constellation Work in the Web.

Lindau, Veit. *Soul on Fire. True Life Manifesto. Wake Up and Live Your Full Potential!* Life Trust, 2012. Kindle edition. Web.

Plotkin, Bill. *Soulcraft: Crossing into the Mysteries of Nature and Psyche*. San Francisco: New World Library, 2010. Print.

Trobe, Krishnananda and Amana Trobe. *Face to Face with Fear: Transforming Fear Into Love*. Cambridge (UK): Perfect Publishers, 2009. Print.

Trobe, Krishnananda and Amana Trobe. *Stepping Out of Fear – Breaking Free of Pain and Suffering*. Minneapolis: Langdon Street Press (Hillcrest), 2009. Print.

Suggested Family Constellation Facilitators

I can recommend with clear conscience the family constellation facilitators shown below. They can assist you on the subject of relationships (as well as many other issues, of course).

Practitioner of the Hellinger School of Constellation Therapy

Gerhard Walper (Bad Homburg, Germany and worldwide)
http://stilles-familienstellen.de/

In the general area of family systemic constellation work

Wolfgang Bracht (Freiburg, Germany)
http://www.wolfgang-bracht.de/

Switzerland

Marion Heine (Basel)
http://www.familienstellen-basel.ch/

USA

Laura Ghedina (Connecticut)
http://lauraghedina.com

More Books on Systemic Family Constellation Work by Marc Baco

Marc Baco

**Stopping The Obesity Pattern
With
Systemic Constellation Work**

Why self-dicipline alone rarely succeeds

Summary

Are you fed up with being seen as lazy and without discipline?

Although you've tried everything, does your excess weight come back like a boomerang?

Have you already given up and resigned yourself to the fact that you will never live in your ideal-sized body?

Systemic Family Constellation Work can help where therapies, diets, and lifestyle changes have not been able to give lasting results.

This book is written for all those affected by excess weight, and for Systemic Constellation facilitators who are helping clients with body weight issues. It's no substitute for a Constellation session, but reading it prepares you to participate in a Systemic Family Constellation.

Some chapters have exercises to do at home that will help you achieve your personal goals to drop excess weight.

Learn from others who have changed their lives and attained their ideal body weight with a Systemic Constellation.

New books by Marc Baco on:
www.37voices.de

The blog for Family Systemic Constellations:
www.marcbaco.de

Made in the USA
Middletown, DE
30 November 2022